# The Sagas of Icelanders

This book offers an accessible and concise introduction to the sagas of Icelanders, perfect for both general and academic readers. Authored by a recognized expert, it immerses readers in the sagas' world, exploring their cultural and historical context. The book surveys major themes such as belief systems, family dynamics, legal matters, honor, and gender roles, elucidating Icelandic society's fundamental worldview. Covering diverse tales from the Middle Ages, the sagas depict the struggles of ordinary farmers, fierce heroes, and shrewd women, including epic expeditions to Greenland and Vinland. The book also examines the influence of foreign literature, manuscript evidence, and dating, categorizing the sagas into three periods. Additionally, it explores their unique literary style, including paranormal elements and skaldic poetry. The final section provides concise summaries and information about the dating, manuscripts, and transmission of the forty preserved sagas, offering a comprehensive understanding of these captivating narratives.

**Annette Lassen** is professor at the Arnamagnæan Collection, NorS, University of Copenhagen. From 2020 to 2022, she was research professor at The Árni Magnússon Institute for Icelandic Studies. She has authored books and articles on Old Icelandic literature such as *Odin's Ways: A Guide to the Pagan God in Medieval Literature* (Routledge 2022) and the edition *Hrafnagaldur Óðins/ Forspjallsljóð* (Viking Society for Northern Research 2011). She has published complete translations in Danish of the sagas of Icelanders and the sagas of ancient times (2014 and 2016–2019).

# Routledge Focus on Literature

**Remapping Energopolitics**
Blue Humanities, Geophilosophy and Sri Lankan Minor Writings
*Abhisek Ghosal*

**Colonial Philippines in Italian Travel Writing**
"Italians" Interpreting Difference
*Jillian Loise Melchor*

**Essays on The Glass Menagerie**
Truth in the Pleasant Disguise of Illusion
*Tania Chakravertty*

**Margaret Wise Brown's Experimental Art**
The Modernist Picture Book
*Julia Pond*

**Tolkien and the Kalevala**
*Jyrki Korpua*

**Elevating Humanity via Africana Womanism**
*Clenora Hudson (Weems)*

**Reading Modernity, Modernism and Religion Today**
Spinoza and Van Gogh
*Patrick Grant*

**The Sagas of Icelanders**
An Introduction to All Forty Sagas with Summaries
*Annette Lassen*

For more information about this series, please visit: www.routledge.com/Routledge-Focus-on-Literature/book-series/RFLT

# The Sagas of Icelanders
An Introduction to All Forty Sagas with Summaries

**Annette Lassen**

Translated and adapted into English by
Marianne Kalinke and Kirsten Wolf

NEW YORK AND LONDON

First published 2025
by Routledge
605 Third Avenue, New York, NY 10158

and by Routledge
4 Park Square, Milton Park, Abingdon, Oxon, OX14 4RN

*Routledge is an imprint of the Taylor & Francis Group, an informa business*

© 2025 Annette Lassen

The right of Annette Lassen to be identified as author of this work has been asserted in accordance with sections 77 and 78 of the Copyright, Designs and Patents Act 1988.

All rights reserved. No part of this book may be reprinted or reproduced or utilised in any form or by any electronic, mechanical, or other means, now known or hereafter invented, including photocopying and recording, or in any information storage or retrieval system, without permission in writing from the publishers.

*Trademark notice*: Product or corporate names may be trademarks or registered trademarks, and are used only for identification and explanation without intent to infringe.

ISBN: 9781032814490 (hbk)
ISBN: 9781032814506 (pbk)
ISBN: 9781003499923 (ebk)

DOI: 10.4324/9781003499923

Typeset in Times New Roman
by codeMantra

# Contents

| | | |
|---|---|---:|
| 1 | Introduction | 1 |
| 2 | Sagas and *Þættir* | 2 |
| 3 | Toward a Definition of the Genre | 3 |
| 4 | Iceland's Literature in the Middle Ages—Influence and Taste | 5 |
| 5 | Transmission | 8 |
| 6 | Age | 11 |
| 7 | Tradition and Narrative | 17 |
| 8 | Saga Writers and Informants | 19 |
| 9 | Icelanders—Nordic Storytellers and Bookworms | 23 |
| 10 | The Historicity of the Sagas of Icelanders | 26 |
| 11 | Style and Literary Technique | 32 |
| 12 | Skaldic Poetry | 40 |
| 13 | The Society of the Sagas of Icelanders | 44 |
| 14 | The Sagas of Icelanders. A Survey | 74 |

*Bard's Saga 74*
*Egil's saga 75*
*Eirik the Red's Saga 76*

vi  *Contents*

*Gisli Sursson's Saga 77*
*Gold-Thorir's Saga 78*
*Hen-Thorir's Saga 79*
*Killer-Glum's Saga 79*
*Kormak's Saga 80*
*Njal's Saga 81*
*Olkofri's Saga 82*
*The Saga of Bjorn, Champion of the Hitardal People 83*
*The Saga of Droplaug's Sons 83*
*The Saga of Finnbogi the Mighty 85*
*The Saga of Grettir the Strong 85*
*The Saga of Gunnar, the Fool of Keldugnup 86*
*The Saga of Gunnlaug Serpent-Tongue 87*
*The Saga of Hallfred the Troublesome Poet 88*
*The Saga of Havard of Isafjord 89*
*The Saga of Hrafnkel Frey's Godi 89*
*The Saga of Hord and the People of Holm 90*
*The Saga of Ref the Sly 91*
*The Saga of the Confederates 91*
*The Saga of the Greenlanders 92*
*The Saga of the People of Eyri 93*
*The Saga of the People of Fljotsdal 94*
*The Saga of the People of Floi 95*
*The Saga of the People of Kjalarnes 96*
*The Saga of the People of Laxardal 96*
*The Saga of the People of Ljosavatn 97*
*The Saga of the People of Reykjadal and of Killer-Skuta 98*
*The Saga of the People of Svarfadardal 98*
*The Saga of the People of Vatnsdal 99*
*The Saga of the People of Vopnafjord 100*
*The Saga of the Slayings on the Heath 101*
*The Saga of the Sworn Brothers 102*
*The Saga of Thord Menace 103*
*The Saga of Thorstein the White 103*
*Thorstein Sidu-Hallsson's Saga 104*
*Valla-Ljot's Saga 105*
*Viglund's Saga 105*

| | |
|---|---|
| *Literature* | *107* |
| *Index* | *113* |
| *Index of Manuscripts* | *119* |

# 1 Introduction

Iceland's saga literature is a Nordic cultural legacy and world literature. One of the best-known groups of sagas is the sagas of Icelanders, powerful narratives about the life of free Icelanders in the late Viking Age. The sagas of Icelanders were recorded over a long period of time in the Middle Ages, and their world is manifold. There are classic and tragic narratives about love, grief, and family feuds; accounts of farmers, who fight one another; tough heroes, shrewd women, trolls, crafty imaginative strategists, and cranky skalds; about fateful expeditions to Greenland and an unknown world (Vinland, contemporary Canada).

The sagas of Icelanders have no parallels in world literature, but they were not composed in cultural isolation in the Middle Ages. The recording of the sagas began around 1200, and the genre took shape in the context of new European cultural currents and the Icelandic narrative tradition about times past.

But the sagas of Icelanders (*Íslendingasögur*) are just one genre of saga literature. There are also sagas of ancient times in the Northern lands (*fornaldarsögur Norðurlanda*), kings' sagas (*konungasögur*), courtly romances (*riddarasögur*), contemporary sagas, bishops' sagas, and apostles' sagas. Moreover, there are other prose texts, which do not belong to saga literature, for example, the *Book of Settlements* (*Landnámabók*) about the colonization of Iceland; Ari the Learned's *Book of Icelanders* (*Íslendingabók*) about early Icelandic history; and Snorri Sturluson's *Edda*, a handbook of skaldic poetry with stories about pagan gods. There are legal texts and scholarly works on grammar, astronomy, calendar reckoning, medicine, and philosophy. Also transmitted are annals or yearbooks, genealogies, charters, sermons, and numerous legends of holy men and women (*heilagra manna sögur*). In short, the Icelandic Middle Ages were a literary melting pot. It was this fruitful encounter of the foreign and indigenous between the learned and the popular that produced Iceland's literary miracle.

The aim of this book is to provide an introduction to the world of the sagas of Icelanders, offering insight into the culture and time of their composition, along with an overview of their key themes and perspectives on the world.

DOI: 10.4324/9781003499923-1

# 2 Sagas and *Þættir*

Internationally, the term "saga" is used for a lengthy epic prose narrative from medieval Iceland, often encompassing a vast array of interconnected characters and events, although some sagas are short and focus on a single conflict. Contrary to the modern usage, the word "saga" has no specific association with saga literature in either Old Icelandic or Modern Icelandic. For the same reason, a saga from the Middle Ages is referred to as an ancient saga in Modern Icelandic (*fornsaga*). In Old Icelandic, the word "saga," which is related to the verb "say" (Icelandic *segja*), simply denotes a story, an account, or an utterance, without distinguishing between written or oral forms.

In contrast to a saga, a *þáttr* (plural *þættir*) is a short story transmitted or embedded in a larger work, a saga, serving as an interlude in the narrative. However, the *þættir* can also be long: The longest *þættir* are longer than the shortest sagas. The original meaning of the word *þáttr* is "strand," suggesting these texts are interwoven parts of a larger narrative rather than independent works. A subgroup of *þættir* (the *þættir* of Icelanders), which have been preserved primarily in the kings' sagas, focuses on the honors and achievements of Icelanders at the foreign courts of mighty kings.

The sagas of Icelanders are often referred to as "Family Sagas," but this is misleading since these sagas do not always focus on a single family. Similarly, designating them "Icelandic Sagas" is confusing since, as mentioned above, there are numerous other Icelandic sagas than the sagas of Icelanders. The sagas of ancient times, the kings' sagas, and the Icelandic courtly sagas were also composed in Iceland, even though they deal with other geographic areas.

DOI: 10.4324/9781003499923-2

# 3 Toward a Definition of the Genre

The sagas of Icelanders depict the lives of affluent farmers in Iceland during the Viking Age. They took place mainly between 930 and 1030, in the so-called Saga Age. The sagas of Icelanders depict the emigration of powerful individuals from Norway and the settlement of Iceland. Some sagas relate that they fled from Norway due to the tyranny of King Harald Fair-hair, while others present a more favorable perspective on Norwegian royal power. Some sagas, such as *Egil's Saga* (*Egils saga Skallagrímssonar*) and *Gisli Sursson's Saga* (*Gisla saga Súrssonar*), focus primarily on one person, while others, such as *The Saga of the People of Vatnsdal* (*Vatnsdæla saga*) and *The Saga of the People of Eyri* (*Eyrbyggja saga*), deal with a specific family or group of people in a distinct geographical area. The plot often revolves around one or more feuds, describing its cause, development, and resolution. This is the case, for example, in *Njal's Saga* (*Brennu-Njáls saga*) and *The Saga of Hrafnkel Frey's Godi* (*Hrafnkels saga Freysgoða*). Some sagas, such as *The Saga of the People of Laxardal* (*Laxdæla saga*), tell of conflicts, not all of which are interrelated. The sagas of Icelanders take place primarily in Iceland, but most sagas give accounts of the travels of young heroic men to Norway, Sweden, England, Ireland, the Orkney Islands, or places farther away. A saga of Icelanders in which one or more heroes don't travel abroad is rare. In contrast, the female protagonists generally remain in Iceland, though a few depart the country for good or go on a pilgrimage, such as Gisli's widow Aud at the conclusion of *Gisli Sursson's Saga*. While abroad, the young man obtains wealth on Viking raids and honor from kings. Typically, he soon becomes a king's confidant or a close friend. After a few years, he becomes homesick, and upon returning to Iceland, conflicts often arise with other farmers over such issues as power, women, land, fishing rights, stranded whales, or the cutting of trees in forests. Sometimes the newly arrived saga hero shows up at the Althing in fine garments he had received from the Norwegian king, and this creates envy among other farmers. In the eighteenth century, Jón Ólafsson from Grunnavík (1705–1779), one of the scribes of Árni Magnússon (1663–1730), the famous manuscript collector, laconically characterized the sagas of Icelanders: Their subject matter is purely and simply

DOI: 10.4324/9781003499923-3

4    *The Sagas of Icelanders*

"farmers fighting each other." In the era of royal absolutism, there was a certain disdain for the lower classes, and there was little or no interest in the honor of those deemed dishonorable. At that time, the focus was on kings' sagas and the sagas of ancient times, which were considered reliable historical sources.

Saga society did not, however, overlook the honor of the farmers. The guiding principle behind the conflicts in the sagas of Icelanders is a protagonist's highly sensitive feeling of honor. One risks losing respect, if a man accidentally rides into one and inflicts a wound, as happens to Gunnar in *Njal's Saga* (Chapter 53). It is an accident, but humiliating, and at first the peace-loving Gunnar takes no action to restore his honor. But when he is derided for having cried, he is compelled to take action. Other offenses are more tangible as when in *The Saga of the People of Laxardal* (Chapter 46) Gudrun coerces her brothers into stealing and burning precious objects belonging to Kjartan, to whom she was once betrothed, but who is now married to another woman. The items are not insignificant: a unique head-dress, given to Kjartan from the Norwegian king's sister as a wedding gift for Gudrun, but presented by him to his wife Hrefna, and a sword, which he had received from the king himself.

The conflicts escalate into bloody family feuds, legal settlements, and juridical prosecutions, but the sagas ultimately conclude with reconciliation and peace. It is not uncommon for minor disputes, instigated by obstreperous individuals, to spark these conflicts. They can originate even among close friends, as is the case in *The Saga of the People of Vopnafjord* (*Vápnfirðinga saga*). It is a general rule in the sagas of Icelanders that an insult must be avenged, as failing to do so would result in the loss of honor. Accordingly, the feuds have a tragic dimension; the heroes are compelled to act, even when they may desire the opposite.

Approximately forty sagas are considered to belong to the group of sagas of Icelanders. Additionally, there are forty-nine *þættir* of Icelanders. All of these works were composed in Iceland during the Middle Ages. Some are written in a concise and pithy style; others are unpolished, raw, and tentative; yet others are fabulous, wild, and unrestrained narratives. Even though the sagas of Icelanders share many stylistic features, they encompass a diverse range of accounts written over a long period with changing literary tastes. The style varies, and the individual saga writers have given the narratives their own individual character.

# 4 Iceland's Literature in the Middle Ages—Influence and Taste

The confluence of the Icelandic narrative tradition and European literary currents is especially evident in *The Saga of the People of Laxardal*, which on the surface appears to be an oral account, but which exhibits clear influences from courtly literature. Occasionally, this saga indicates its written nature in phrases such as "as written above."

In the course of the twelfth century, Europeans began to write comprehensive narratives. To this period belongs, for example, *Historia regum Britanniae* ("History of the British Kings") by Geoffrey of Monmouth (ca. 1100–1155), which blends fact and fiction, as well as Chrétien de Troyes's romances about King Arthur and his knights (from the end of the twelfth century). The courtly literature and romances cultivated the ideal of a chivalric and courtly deportment, that is, one cultivated, sophisticated, and noble. It did not take long before the new literary currents reached Scandinavia. It is believed that Geoffrey of Monmouth's work served as a model for Saxo's *Gesta Danorum* ("History of the Danes") from around 1200, which was also known in Iceland in the Middle Ages. In 1226, the monk Brother Robert translated the saga of Tristram and Ísǫnd from the Old French *Tristran* into Old Norse at the request of the Norwegian King Haakon Haakonsson (r. 1217–1263). In 1936, the literary historian Paul V. Rubow claimed that Brother Robert's translation initiated the entire production of sagas in Iceland. Nowadays, scholars do not agree with his theory, yet no one doubts that the translated romances were very important. Indeed, it would be strange, if the Icelanders had not drawn inspiration from French courtly romances in the composition of their sagas.

The oldest preserved Icelandic literary work is Ari the Learned's *Book of Icelanders* from ca. 1120. The work gives a brief survey of the discovery and settlement of Iceland from ca. 870 to 930. It describes the establishment of juridical and ecclesiastical institutions, but in connection with these Ari also mentions events described in the sagas of Icelanders. Toward the end of the twelfth century, Icelandic monks at Þingeyrar, a Benedictine monastery in Northern Iceland, began to write sagas about Norwegian kings. The oldest saga is believed to have been composed at Þingeyrar; this is the monk Oddr Snorrason's *Saga of Olaf*

*Figure 4.1* The person who wrote *Njal's Saga* was well-read and knew among other works the saga about Alexander the Great (*Alexanders saga*). Gunnar's famous words in Chapter 75, "So lovely is the hillside that it has never before seemed to me as lovely as now, with its pale fields and mown meadows …" are believed to derive from *Alexander's Saga*, when Alexander looks out over Asia. *Alexander's Saga* is to the left (the passage begins in the first column on the left leaf, l. 22). *Njal's Saga* is to the right (the passage begins on the right leaf, l. 10). AM 226 fol. (ca. 1350–1360) and AM 468 4to (Reykjabók, ca. 1300–1325), The Arnamagnaean Collection, University of Copenhagen. Photo: Suzanne Reitz.

*Tryggvason* (*Óláfs saga Tryggvasonar*). The earliest kings' sagas were written in Latin, but they were soon translated into Old Norse. Oddr's Latin original has been lost, but it is preserved in an Old Norse/Icelandic translation. It was not until then that the sagas of Icelanders were composed.

In the past, scholars believed that it was possible to detect a change in taste in the development of the sagas of Icelanders. The oldest sagas of Icelanders were supposed to be characterized by a primitive or even style, as is the case in *The Saga of the Slayings on the Heath* (*Heiðarvíga saga*). In time, the style developed and became artistically perfected, as witnessed by *Njal's Saga* and *The Saga of Hrafnkel Frey's Godi*. After Iceland's loss of independence in 1262, the style was thought to have degenerated under the influence of foreign literature. Accordingly, the youngest sagas have sometimes been referred to as "bastards" in older scholarship. This theory has been called "the decay theory," according to which the quality of the sagas is closely tied to political circumstances

## Iceland's Literature in the Middle Ages—Influence and Taste   7

in Iceland. According to this theory, recessions produce bad literature, while times of prosperity produce good literature. At the end of the nineteenth century, researchers also were of the opinion that the better a saga of Icelanders was, the older it had to be. But it is worth considering that the question of taste and style is difficult when dealing with texts that are 600–800 years old, because one may unintentionally judge the sagas based on contemporary tastes. Quite simply, it makes little sense to speak of a degeneration of literary taste in Iceland after 1262. In the late Middle Ages, there was a taste for fast-paced and grotesque narratives. This is also evident in fourteenth-century English and Italian works by Geoffrey Chaucer (ca. 1340–1400) and Giovanni Boccaccio (1313–1375). But in Oddr Snorrason's *Saga of Olaf Tryggvason*, a taste for the fantastic can already be detected, and even though there is a rational tendency in some thirteenth-century works, most clearly in *Heimskringla* (*Disc of the World*), this does not at all apply to all works of this period. It should also be noted that foreign literary influence is not only a late medieval phenomenon: Even before the sagas began to be composed, there was a significant influx of literary currents from Europe to Iceland. After the conversion to Christianity, many religious and theological works were written, including narratives about the life and death of saints (*vitae* and *passiones*, respectively). Soon after the conversion to Christianity, wealthy Icelandic farmers sent their sons abroad for education, where they became acquainted with recent contemporary literature. In the beginning of the twelfth century, the first bishop in the north of Iceland, Jón Qgmundarson (1052–1121), established a school in the bishopric of Hólar. Here prospective priests received an education in the seven liberal arts: the trivium (grammar, logic, and rhetoric), along with the quadrivium (geometry, arithmetic, astronomy, and music). Little is known about the school's library, but *The Saga of St. Jón of Hólar* (*Jóns saga helga*), relates that Bishop Jón once caught a young man, Klœngr Þorsteinsson (1102–1176), reading Ovid's *Ars amatoria* (*Art of love*). Klœngr later became bishop of Skálholt in the south of Iceland. The authors of the sagas were monks and were educated. Libraries and reading in schools and monasteries in Iceland and abroad influenced future priests and potential saga writers. Indeed, there are passages in the sagas of Icelanders, which have their origin in learned theological works. An example is Flosi's dream in *Njal's Saga*, which has been traced to Gregory's *Dialogues* (from 593 to 594), a collection of narratives about miracles and saints in the form of a dialogue. In *Njal's Saga*, Flosi dreams that an unknown man emerges from a cliff and calls out the names of men who are soon doomed to die. In Gregory's work, the monk Anastasius hears a voice from a cliff shouting the names of eight of his fellow monks, who all die the next day. And a somewhat obscene passage in the late medieval *Saga of Grettir the Strong* (*Grettis saga sterka*), where Grettir demonstrates his sexual prowess to an unimpressed maid by raping her, is believed to have been inspired by one of the stories in Giovanni Boccaccios's *Decameron.*

# 5 Transmission

It is impossible to give a precise dating of the sagas of Icelanders. The authors of the sagas are unknown, and thus scholars are left to rely on the transmission of manuscripts, among other things, for discovering the age of the sagas. Moreover, the majority of the scribes are anonymous, and one must count on a fifty-year margin of error for dating the manuscripts. The dating is made difficult by gaps in the transmission of the sagas. Over the centuries, many manuscripts have been lost, and the existing manuscripts do not tell the full story. Moreover, not a single original manuscript of a saga has been preserved. The sagas of Icelanders have been transmitted in copies and in copies of copies. Accordingly, the date of the manuscripts does not necessarily reflect the age of the saga. In some cases, a saga is preserved in manuscripts believed to be approximately contemporaneous with the composition of the saga. In other cases, a saga is preserved exclusively in much younger manuscripts from after the Middle Ages, and of some sagas there are only fragments. Worst of all, medieval manuscripts provide titles of sagas that have been completely lost. In a famous manuscript from around 1350 (Möðruvallabók), there is a note on an otherwise blank leaf between *Njal's Saga* and *Egil's Saga*: "Make sure that Gauk Thrandilsson's saga is written here; I have heard that Mr. Grim has it." But the saga was never recorded in this manuscript, and it has not been transmitted.

The oldest fragment of a saga of Icelanders is the so-called theta-fragment of *Egil's Saga* from around 1250. From the end of the thirteenth century, there are fragments of *The Saga of the People of Laxardal* and *The Saga of the People of Eyri*, but manuscripts of complete sagas of Icelanders are not extant until around 1300. From this time on, a larger number of saga manuscripts is extant. Three manuscripts of *Njal's Saga* from around 1300 have been preserved: Reykjabók, Gráskinna, and Kálfalækjabók.

It is believed that only ten percent of the manuscripts that once existed have been preserved. The transmission of *The Saga of the Slayings on the Heath* illustrates the perilous journey of manuscripts over the centuries. In the eighteenth century, a medieval parchment of the saga was in Sweden. By that time, the conclusion of the saga was already missing. Árni Magnússon borrowed the manuscript in order to have it copied in Copenhagen by the aforenamed Jón Ólafsson from Grunnavík. Both the parchment and Jón Ólafsson's copy perished in the fire in Copenhagen in 1728. Jón Ólafsson subsequently reconstructed the saga from memory and a list of words that he had compiled on the basis of the saga, which is all that is left of this part of the saga today. Fortunately, the Swedes had forgotten to lend Árni Magnússon the last part of the saga (from Chapter 15), ensuring that this part survived and was rediscovered in Sweden at the end of the eighteenth century. Although a single leaf was missing, it was discovered in the twentieth century in the National Library of Iceland in Reykjavík.

Some sagas have been transmitted only fragmentarily in medieval manuscripts. This is the case of *The Saga of the People of Eyri* and *The Saga of Bjorn, Champion of the Hitardal People* (*Bjarnar saga Hítdœlakappa*). *The Saga of the People of Eyri* is preserved in its entirety only in post-medieval manuscripts, and portions of *The Saga of Bjorn* are missing. One saga that has been preserved solely in post-medieval manuscripts is *The Saga of the People of Fljotsdal* (*Fljótsdœla saga*). The oldest fragment of this saga is dated to the beginning of the seventeenth century; the conclusion of the saga is lost. Even though the saga is preserved only in young manuscripts, scholars believe that it was composed in the Middle Ages.

There are also sagas, which have been transmitted in many manuscripts, and which are found in more than one redaction, such as *Gisli Sursson's Saga* and *Egil's Saga*. *Gisli Sursson's Saga* has been transmitted in both a shorter and a longer redaction, and there exists a fragment of a third redaction. *Egil's Saga* is preserved in three redactions, called the A-, B-, and C-redactions. The three redactions differ in regard to Egil's poems and religion. The A-redaction contains the most copious prose text and includes most of Egil's *lausavísur* ("loose verses" or situational verses), but neither the poems *Head Ransom* (*Hǫfuðlausn*) nor *Loss of Sons* (*Sonatorrek*). The B-redaction contains *Head Ransom*, but not *Loss of Sons*. Nor does the B-redaction contain all the *lausavísur*. The C-redaction, which is considered to be a late-medieval redaction, contains both *Head Ransom* and *Loss of Sons*.

The A-redaction of *Egil's Saga* is preserved in the manuscript Möðruvallabók from around 1350. The manuscript contains a large collection of sagas of Icelanders: *Njal's Saga, Egil's Saga, The Saga of Finnbogi the Mighty* (*Finnboga saga ramma*), *The Saga of the Confederates* (*Bandamanna saga*), *Kormak's saga* (*Kormáks saga*), *Killer-Glum's saga* (*Víga-Glúms saga*), *The Saga of Droplaug's Sons* (*Droplaugarsona saga*), *Olkofri's Saga* (*Ǫlkofra saga*), *The Saga of Hallfred the Troublesome Poet* (*Hallfreðar saga vandrœðaskálds*), *The Saga of the People of Laxardal, Bolli Bollason's Tale* (*Bolla þáttr Bollasonar*), and *The Saga of the Sworn Brothers* (*Fóstbrœðra saga*). As Jóhanna Katrín Friðriksdóttir (2020) has argued, the manuscript's exclusive focus on the sagas of Icelanders cannot be taken as evidence that, in fourteenth-century Iceland, the sagas of Icelanders were considered a genre. Most of the manuscripts are with

*Figure 5.1* From four defective leaves we have knowledge of a third redaction of *Gisli Sursson's Saga*. The leaves, originally belonging to a vellum manuscript, were at one point cut and used as binding for another book. AM 445 c I 4to (ca. 1390–1425), The Árni Magnússon Institute for Icelandic Studies, Reykjavík. Photo: Jóhanna Ólafsdóttir.

varying content. As far as is known, the designation *Íslendingasögur*, "sagas of Icelanders," to refer to a specific genre was not used in the Middle Ages. The term is found only in one medieval source, *Óláfsmáldagi* ("Olaf's inventory"), a charter (a document with legal validity) dated 1461, which provides a catalogue of books. Here, mention is made of "a bad saga of Icelanders"; doubtlessly, this refers to the poor state of the manuscript and not to the literary quality of the saga. Moreover, it is possible that the reference is to Sturla Þórðarson's (1214–1284) *Saga of Icelanders* (*Íslendinga saga*), a contemporary saga.

# 6 Age

Although it is impossible to date the sagas of Icelanders with certainty, most scholars agree that they began to be written in the first half of the thirteenth century. The production of sagas continued throughout the Middle Ages with adaptations and revisions of existing sagas and new compositions. The dating of the individual sagas continues to be debated. The oldest sagas of Icelanders are considered to be somewhat younger than the oldest kings' sagas, which are considered the oldest group of sagas. *The Saga of the Slayings on the Heath* is often regarded as the oldest saga of Icelanders, and traditionally it has been dated to around 1200. Scholars have typically regarded the earliest composition of the sagas of Icelanders as contemporaneous with Snorri Sturluson's (1179–1241) *Edda* and *Heimskringla*. Snorri's *Edda* has generally been dated to around 1220 and *Heimskringla* to 1230. Some scholars, however, have doubted Snorri's authorship of *Heimskringla* as the work is transmitted in the famous manuscript Kringla, arguing that Sturla Þórðarson is behind this redaction. In addition, there is a persistent theory that Snorri is the writer of *Egil's Saga*. The theory has recently been revived by Haukur Þorgeirsson, accompanied by new arguments.

When on rare occasions a saga refers to known individuals from the Middle Ages, this can be used to help date the saga. An example is the mention in *The Saga of the People of Eyri* of Snorri Sturluson and his brothers. The saga writer must have known Snorri and his brothers—unless a later writer added the note to an older text available to him. *The Saga of the People of Laxardal* refers to "Ketil, abbot of Helgafell;" Ketil was appointed abbot in 1217, and therefore one can surmise that the saga was not written before that. But later scribes might have altered or added this information in their copies or adaptations of the saga.

Many of the individuals named in the sagas of Icelanders appear in more than one saga, and it is evident that some sagas borrowed from other sagas. In such cases, it is possible to establish an inner chronology between and among the sagas. However, borrowings provide no real assistance when it comes to dating the sagas. A few sagas make direct mention of other sagas. *The Saga of the People of Eyri* mentions *The Saga of the People of Laxardal* and *The*

DOI: 10.4324/9781003499923-6

12　*The Sagas of Icelanders*

*Saga of the Slayings on the Heath*, and *The Saga of Grettir the Strong* mentions *The Saga of the Confederates*. There is also a close connection between several sagas of Icelanders and the *Book of Settlements*. A number of the saga writers used Sturla Þórðarson's (1214–1284) redaction of the *Book of Settlements* (*Sturlubók*), which he wrote between 1240 and 1284, as an exemplar for their saga. In the *Book of Settlements*, the writers could find information about names, family relations, land-taking, and in this work they could read saga-like passages about the first settlers. The saga writers often expanded upon the information in the *Book of Settlements* or added elements from other texts. Some sagas of Icelanders also deal with fictitious descendants of known settlers, as is the case in *Bard's Saga* (*Bárðar saga Snæfellsáss*). But in his redaction of the *Book of Settlements*, Sturla Þórðarson also drew on information in the sagas of Icelanders. Traditionally, scholars have not considered these passages to align sufficiently with the transmitted sagas of Icelanders to suggest that Sturla could have used them in the form known today. Sturla recounts passages from four late medieval sagas, *The Saga of Hord and the People of Holm* (*Harðar saga ok Hólmverja*), *The Saga of Havard of Isafjord* (*Hávarðar saga Ísfirðings*), *The Saga of the People of Svarfadardal* (*Svarfdæla saga*), and *Gold-Thorir's Saga* (*Gull-Þóris saga*). Most scholars have therefore been of the opinion that the transmitted sagas are younger adaptations of older, now lost versions, and that it was the older versions to which Sturla had access. But recently, Daniel Sävborg (2012) has argued against this, suggesting that we don't know when the supposedly late additions became part of the sagas as we have them now.

Attempts to date the sagas have been compared to building a house of cards. It sometimes does not take long before a hypothesis about the age of a saga is contradicted. Despite disagreements about the dating of individual sagas, they can roughly be divided into three groups according to their age. It must be emphasized, however, that the division should be taken with a grain of salt, since it relies on uncertain datings. With arguments from one scholar a saga can move from the oldest group to the youngest, or vice versa, as has happened with *The Saga of Grettir the Strong* and *The Saga of the Sworn Brothers*.

**The Oldest Period**

The oldest group of sagas consists of:

> *The Saga of the Slayings on the Heath* (1200)
> *Eirik the Red's Saga (Eiríks saga rauða)* (1200–1230)
> *The Saga of Droplaug's Sons* (1200–1240)
> *The Saga of Bjorn, Champion of the Hitardal People* (1215–1230)
> *Egil's Saga* (1220–1230)
> *The Saga of Hallfred the Troublesome Poet* (1220)
> *Kormak's saga* (1220)

*Figure 6.1* The Saga of the Sworn Brothers in the manuscript Hauksbók. The beginning of the saga is lost in this manuscript and the saga abbreviated. As can be seen the parchment, the dried and stretched calfskin on which the saga is written, is damaged. AM 544 4to (ca. 1300). The Arnamagnæan Collection, University of Copenhagen. Photo: Suzanne Reitz.

*Valla-Ljot's Saga (Valla-Ljóts saga)* (1220–1240)
*The Saga of the People of Vopnafjord* (1225–1250)
*The Saga of the People of Ljosavatn (Ljósvetninga saga)* (1230–1250)
*Thorstein Sidu-Hallsson's Saga (Þorsteins saga Síðu-Hallssonar)* (1250)
*Olkofri's Saga* (1250)
*The Saga of the People of Reykjadal and of Killer-Skuta (Reykdæla saga ok Víga-Skútu)* (1250)

There is particular uncertainty regarding the dating of two sagas:

*The Saga of the Greenlanders (Grænlendinga saga)* (1200–1230 or 1300)
*The Saga of the Sworn Brothers* (1200 or 1300)

*The Saga of the Sworn Brothers* is transmitted in three different redactions with great stylistic differences. The oldest of these includes some learned digressions, for example about anatomy and geography. The style in these learned additions is very different from what one otherwise finds in the sagas of Icelanders, and scholars have not agreed on the purpose of these digressions. In the saga, a man

14    *The Sagas of Icelanders*

called Egil is terrified when he is being chased by armed men and shakes with fear when he is caught. Then, an interpolation on anatomy reads as follows:

> Every bone in his body shook, all two hundred and fourteen of them. All his teeth chattered, and there were thirty of them. And all the veins in his skin trembled with fear, and there were four hundred and fifteen of them.
>
> (Chapter 24)

It is difficult not to smile and, indeed, the passage has been regarded by some as a reflection of a poor or degenerate (learned) taste or humor on the part of the saga writer and therefore as evidence that the saga belongs to the period of decay around 1300. However, the passage has also been interpreted as an expression of the incipient development of saga style, and that the saga writer wanted to use the opportunity to educate his readers or listeners about anatomy. Accordingly, the saga has been dated to the very earliest period around 1200, when it was probably written in close connection with *The Saga of Saint Olaf* (*Óláfs saga helga*).

The oldest sagas in the early group are characterized by a style that can be considered simple, with occasional elements that may seem unrefined or uneven. They may appear to be raw recordings of events, and it is easy to imagine how an Icelander with antiquarian interests in his (or his patron's) district, his family's, or his country's history, attempted to tackle this raw material. But a simple or unrefined style is, of course, not necessarily an indication of age. To the oldest group belong also polished and consummate works, such as *Egil's Saga*. To this group belong also other skald sagas, all of which are closely connected to the kings' sagas, since they have a king's Icelandic skald as the principal character.

**The Middle Period**

The sagas belonging to the middle period comprise:

*The Saga of the People of Eyri* (1220–1265)
*The Saga of the People of Laxardal* (ca. 1230–1260)
*Gisli Sursson's Saga* (ca. 1250)
*The Saga of the Confederates* (ca. 1250)
*Hen-Thorir's Saga (Hænsa-Þóris saga)* (ca. 1250–1270)
*The Saga of Gunnlaug Serpent-Tongue (Gunnlaugs saga ormstungu)* (ca. 1270–1280)
*The Saga of the People of Vatnsdal* (ca. 1270–1280)
*Killer-Glum's saga* (ca. 1270–1280)
*The Saga of Thorstein the White (Þorsteins saga hvíta)* (1275–1300)
*Njal's Saga* (ca. 1280)
*The Saga of Hrafnkel Frey's Godi* (ca. 1300)

*Age* 15

The sagas in this group are often referred to as "classical" sagas, since it is believed that during this period the art of saga writing reached its zenith. These sagas of Icelanders have more or less distinct fictional features and some of them are fiction from beginning to end, such as *The Saga of Hrafnkel Frey's Godi*. Some of the sagas in this group also contain unmistakable historical features, but in contrast to the oldest group it is now obvious that an artist was at work. The saga writers are conscious of structure and form: The beginning of *Gisli Sursson's Saga* hints at the plot, which then unfolds to perfection in the saga's main action. The best of the sagas in the middle period have been praised not only for their perfected composition, but also for their lucid language and vivid depictions of persons and psychology. The conflicts in these sagas are not black and white. The most famous of these sagas is *Njal's Saga*. In his lectures at the University of Copenhagen in 1848–1849, Professor Carsten Hauch demonstrated that "an aesthetic vision" is evident in *Njal's Saga*. Indeed, Hauch's lectures on *Njal's Saga* became a starting point for a new view of the sagas of Icelanders as literature and not historiography.

**The Youngest Period**

The sagas which belong to the late medieval period are:

> *The Saga of the People of Floi (Flóamanna saga)* (1290–1330)
> *The Saga of Finnbogi the Mighty* (1300–1350)
> *Gold-Thorir's Saga* (1300–1350)
> *The Saga of Havard of Isafjord* (1300–1350)
> *The Saga of Hord and the People of Holm* (1300–1400)
> *The Saga of the People of Kjalarnes (Kjalnesinga saga)* (1310–1320)
> *The Saga of Ref the Sly (Króka-Refs saga)* (1325–1375)
> *The Saga of Thord Menace (Þórðar saga hreðu)* (1350)
> *Bard's Saga* (1350–1380)
> *The Saga of the People of Svarfadardal* (1350–1400)
> *Viglund's Saga (Víglundar saga)* (1400)
> *The Saga of Gunnar, the Fool of Keldugnup (Gunnars saga Keldugnúpsfífls)*
> (1400–1500)

About the dating of two sagas there has been considerable disagreement:

> *The Saga of the People of Fljotsdal* (1300–1400 or 1500–1550)
> *The Saga of Grettir the Strong* (1310–1320 or 1400)

Recently, Daniel Sävborg has argued that *Gold-Thorir's Saga*, *The Saga of Havard of Isafjord*, *The Saga of Hord and the People of Holm*, and *The Saga of the People of Svarfadardal* were composed before 1280 (2012).

16  *The Sagas of Icelanders*

The sagas in this group are generally considered to have been inspired by the more fantastic, or in a modern historical sense, unreliable sagas of ancient times. But one must bear in mind that fantastic elements do not provide a reliable basis for dating: Some historical works from around 1200 contain fantastic elements, as is evident, for example, in Oddr Snorrason's *Saga of Olaf Tryggvason* and Saxo Grammaticus' *History of the Danes*. Some of the titles of the sagas in this group indicate that the taste tends toward the grotesque and exaggerated—at a high artistic level. *The Saga of Gunnar, the Fool of Keldugnup* is both as amusing and unserious as it sounds; not to mention *The Saga of Ref the Sly*, where we encounter a cunning and skilled inventor who could arouse the envy of the smartest engineer with his imaginative constructions. In the younger sagas, there is also a greater interest in heathen practices than in the older sagas. The same tendencies can be detected in other sagas and *þættir*, which have been dated to this period, for example, in Flateyjarbók, the largest manuscript of all, dated to ca. 1387–1395. A characteristic of this period is that the sagas appear to a greater extent to have been written as fiction and for entertainment. Many of these sagas are short, quick-paced, and lively with at times an intense and coarse sense of humor. The saga writers juggle with stereotypes from the older sagas of Icelanders and often provide skillful entertainment.

But it is not only fun and entertainment. A number of the late sagas have tragic dimensions, not least *The Saga of the People of Floi*, which, by the way, is also a reflection of Bernadine theology. To this group belongs also the extraordinarily interesting trolls' saga: *Bard's Saga*, which explores brutality toward one's own family, which according to the inner logic of the saga is especially heathen. In this group of sagas, a few Nordic gods now also appear. In the *Saga of Hord and the People of Holm*, Odin helps the hero open a burial mound, and in the *Bard's Saga* Odin preaches paganism to a priest, who ends up smacking him on the head with his crucifix. In *The Saga of the People of Floi*, Thor appears lifelike in a series of dreams, and he is responsible for the many misfortunes that befall that ill-fated Icelandic expedition to Greenland.

# 7　Tradition and Narrative

Much of the research on the sagas of Icelanders in the twentieth century has dealt with the relationship between oral tradition and the written saga. Scholarship on the sagas of Icelanders was for a long time dominated by two directions, which the Swiss scholar Andreas Heusler named freeprose theory and bookprose theory. While freeprose theory emphasizes the sagas' oral tradition and argues that the sagas existed as firm oral narratives before they were committed to writing, bookprose theory maintains that sagas are a written product. For a long time, it was believed that the oral narratives preserved authentic stories from the past, but we now know that oral as well as written narratives can be invented from nothing. The bookprose theory does not reject the possibility that there has been or may have been an oral background for the written saga, but stresses that the sagas are written works of art. Most scholars now agree that the truth must be sought somewhere between these two points of view.

Recently, some scholars have argued that the sagas of Icelanders may be regarded as an expression of cultural memory, that the sagas of Icelanders create continuity in the sense that they connect the saga writers' past and present. The saga writers often reflect on traces of the past in the landscape of the present. An example is found in *The Saga of the People of Svarfadardal*, which states that "remnants […] can still be seen [of the assemblies]" (Chapter 10). The past is here rooted in the present landscape.

There is hardly any doubt that in the Middle Ages, the greater part of the sagas were regarded as historical accounts of past heroes—perhaps a bit like the historical novels we know today, where a writer invents a story with fictitious dialogues and feelings around a more or less complete framework of historical facts. But there is not always a historical kernel, and the oral aspects can easily deceive us. In 1940, the Icelandic professor Sigurður Nordal was able to demonstrate that *The Saga of Hrafnkel Frey's Godi* was invented from beginning to end. Until then, *The Saga of Hrafnkel Frey's Godi* had long been regarded as an unusually good and reliable historical source. The saga deals with the Frey-worshipper Hrafnkel's power, his fall, humiliation, and rehabilitation. It is short and concise and therefore easy to remember, and it does not contain any exaggerations or

DOI: 10.4324/9781003499923-7

# 18    *The Sagas of Icelanders*

supernatural elements. Earlier research believed that the saga had existed and been transmitted orally in an almost complete form until it was committed to writing in the Middle Ages without significant alterations. But in his slender and immensely influential book *Hrafnkatla,* Sigurður Nordal convincingly argued that *The Saga of Hrafnkel Frey's Godi* is the work of an artist and a fictional novel. The Saga differs from other sagas of Icelanders in several ways. *The Saga of Hrafnkel Frey's Godi* is unusually coherent; essentially, it deals with only one conflict and only eight individuals, and women hardly appear (only three women are named). Sigurður Nordal called the saga both "unromantic" and a "man's saga." Among other things, he demonstrated that the saga writer knew the *Book of Settlements*, but contradicted its information, and by comparing the saga with other sources, he showed how in the Saga Age there simply was no place for Thorgeir Thjostarsson's chieftaincy (*goðorð*), that is, his juridical and religious office, in Thorskafjord, never mind Hrafnkel's chieftaincy in Fljotsdal, and that Thorgeir and Thorkel never existed. Sigurður Nordal also noted that the saga is extraordinarily detailed in descriptions of nature, weather, and the appearance of individuals—elements which, according to him, cannot have come from oral tradition. Moreover, the descriptions of the landscape in the saga do not agree with the actual geography: below Hrafnkel's farm Adalbol there was supposedly the crag Freyfaxahamar from which the horse was pushed—but in reality, the landscape there is flat. Sigurður Nordal's conclusion was that the events related in the saga never took place. Accordingly, *The Saga of Hrafnkel Frey's Godi* is no more trustworthy as a historical source than *Bard's Saga*, which deals with trolls in Iceland. Its style is just more realistic.

The sagas of Icelanders easily deceive their readers because they give the impression that they transmit an oral tradition apart of the written saga and demand to be read as historical narratives. Via stereotypical formulas, the sagas tempt their readers to believe that they are oral narratives. The sagas use expressions such as "it is told," "one tells," "most people say," "some are of the opinion," and so forth, which at least on the surface give the impression that the writer is a mediator of what in his time is a well-known tradition concerning the events about which he is writing. In the oldest sagas, this may be genuine, but one must take into account that at some point in the fourteenth century, or earlier, references to oral transmission became characteristic of saga style, and in the late medieval sagas of Icelanders such allusions may be inventions by the writer.

# 8 Saga Writers and Informants

Because of the saga writers' anonymity, the immediate circumstances surrounding the origin of the sagas of Icelanders are unknown. A saga writer could work both as an artist, who added elements without basis in known tradition, and as an historian, who recorded the material to which he had access and tried to make it correspond to what he believed was the truth. Often, one must imagine a collective of saga writers behind a saga. It is probable that in a number of cases saga writers early on had available to them oral narratives and later on also written accounts. But with a view to a good story, saga writers adapted the existing material; they revised earlier texts, and in many instances, they made up matter on the basis of events in their own time. They could freely take and use what they wanted from oral narratives or written texts. The notion of copyright did not exist until the technology to copy mechanically was invented.

Nonetheless, the saga writers sometimes reveal a little bit about the transmission and origin of their saga. At the end of *The Saga of Droplaug's Sons*, which has been preserved in a manuscript from ca. 1350, there is a unique piece of information about the origin of the saga:

> Helga lived on at Arneidarstadir after Ingjald's death, as did Thorkel, the son of her and Grim. Thorvald had a son whose name was Ingjald. It was his son, named Thorvald, who told this story. It was one year after Thangbrand the priest came to Iceland that Helgi Droplaugarson fell.
>
> (Chapter 15)

Thorvald, who told the saga, is a descendant of one of the saga's heroes. Unfortunately, it is impossible to precisely determine the timespan of Thorvald's life because there is an error in the text (either the first "Thorvald" mentioned is a mistake for "Thorkel" or vice versa, or else some generation is missing. Still, the information is important because it shows that in the fourteenth century it was considered likely that sagas were transmitted within a family.

20   *The Sagas of Icelanders*

*The Saga of the People of Eyri* too includes a reference to an informant and an eyewitness, since it relates that at a later time the saga heroes' bones were transferred to a newly established church, which was still there in the saga writer's lifetime:

> When this happened Gudny Bodvarsdottir was present, and she is the mother of Sturla's sons Snorri, Thord and Sighvat, and she reported that they were the bones of a medium-sized man, and not a tall one. She also said that the bones of Bork the Stout, Snorri the Godi's uncle, were moved at the same time, and they were extremely large. The bones of the old woman, Thordis, the daughter of Thorbjorn Sur and the mother of Snorri the Godi, were also moved, and Gudny said they were small female bones, and as black as if they had been singed. All of these bones were reburied in the graveyard where the church now stands.
>
> (Chapter 65)

The events of the saga are here connected to the Sturlungs, an especially powerful, famous family, which also included writers. The first of the three sons mentioned is none other than Snorri Sturluson, the man behind the *Edda* and *Heimskringla*. The saga, or at least this paragraph, must have been written after Sturla's three sons had become famous.

It is known that another member of the Sturlung family, Snorri's nephew Sturla Þórðarson, played a significant role in the creation of the sagas of Icelanders. As mentioned above (p. 12), he was behind a redaction of the *Book of Settlements*, which was used by many saga writers. He is also mentioned in a seventeenth-century manuscript of *The Saga of Grettir the Strong*, in which the scribe notes that the manuscript is a copy of the version, which "we believe Sturla Þórðarson compiled." This does not necessarily mean that Sturla is the writer, but the possibility cannot be excluded. In medieval manuscripts, he was also associated with the saga as an authority on Grettir:

> Sturla the Lawspeaker has said that he does not consider any outlaw to have been as distinguished as Grettir the Strong, and justifies this on three grounds. Firstly, he regards him as the wisest, since he spent the longest time in outlawry of any man and was never overcome for as long as he kept his health. Secondly, he was the strongest man in Iceland among his contemporaries, and more capable than others at laying revenants and hauntings to rest. The third reason was that, unlike any other Icelander, he was avenged in Constantinople.
>
> (Chapter 93)

The saga writer does not pronounce his own judgment on Grettir but refers instead to someone considered an expert in history. In the same way, *The Saga of Gunnlaug Serpent-Tongue* begins with a note claiming that Ari Þorgilsson, who wrote the *Book of Icelanders*, is the writer:

> This is the saga of Hrafn and of Gunnlaug Serpent-tongue, as told by the priest Ari Thorgilsson the Learned, who was most knowledgeable about stories of the settlement and other ancient lore of anyone to have lived in Iceland.
>
> (Preface to the saga)

Scholars now agree that Ari the Learned was not behind the extant version of *The Saga of Gunnlaug Serpent-Tongue*. But the possibility that he wrote an older version of the saga cannot be discounted.

Sometimes a saga writer complains about a lack of information. In such cases, it seems that he had more, or more reliable information about other events available to him, when he wrote the saga. The writer of *The Saga of the People of Reykjadal and Killer-Skuta* honestly admits that he lacks certain pieces of information:

> We are not able to report reliably on the circumstances of the deaths of these men, but we know this was Skuta's first revenge for Askel the Godi, his father.
>
> (Chapter 19)

One can imagine that a conscientious historian would write in this way. There are also other features of the sagas of Icelanders which appear to have their origin in a historian's methodology: often there are more people than the narrative needs; kinship relations and relationships by marriage often seem unnecessarily complicated; and finally, there are lengthy genealogies. Scholars have attributed these elements to a lack of freedom on the part of the saga writers concerning an existing tradition. This becomes clear when a saga writer mentions conflicting traditions. In *The Saga of the People of Reykjadal and Killer-Skuta* one reads:

> It is said that at this point the ice bridge broke beneath Steingrim and his men. Some claim Vemund shot Steingrim with a spear when he tried to come up through a hole in the ice and that caused his death and some say he drowned there in the hole.
>
> (Chapter 16)

*The Saga of the People of Svarfadardal* also refers to conflicting traditions. Evidently, the saga writer did not know which was correct, but he carefully mentions the traditions of which he knew:

> Karl remained at Upsir his entire life, and in some people's version he travelled abroad and continued his family line, but many others say that he married Ragnhild, Ljotolf's daughter, and had many children with her.
>
> (Chapter 27)

22    *The Sagas of Icelanders*

Other passages in *The Saga of the People of Svarfadardal* testify to the fact that our modern perception of the nature of a historical account is anachronistic when dealing with medieval texts. When the worst villain in the valley has finally been killed, he begins to haunt and continues to involve himself in the conflict, and he uses his own chopped-off head to knock on people's doors. And in the concluding abominable and in every way misogynistic disciplining of Yngvild Fair-Cheek (whom one as reader does not care for either), one detects influence from the violent punishment of unruly women known in Iceland from the romances, not least *The Saga of Klarus* (*Clári saga*). It is because of Yngvild Fair-Cheek's obstinacy and pride that there is no reconciliation among the saga's warring clans. She is tough and cold and does not show any emotion when her three sons are beheaded before her eyes. Not until she has been sold several times as a slave and she returns, beaten and raped, is her pride broken. But then her husband no longer wants her, and the saga writer comments that "no one knows whether she got married, but some say that in despair she took her own life" (Chapter 29). The saga writer appears to regard the story about Yngvild Fair-Cheek as true, unless he is here playing to the gallery. However, this is probably not the case, since the saga writer also mentions that many people are descended from Karl the Young, who is Yngvild's worst tormentor. Indeed, toward the end of the saga, he expresses a certain caution, which suggests that he probably did not think that he was passing on lies and false rumors:

> We think that Bodvar, the son of Eyjolf Broad-head, lived at Urdir, from whom the people of Urdir are descendants. [...] There are many stories of Valla-Ljot, or Ljot of the farm Vellir, who was a great chieftain.
>
> (My emphasis; Chapter 27)

In such places, one can almost catch the saga writers, with the quill in their hands, considering their doubts and uncertainties, their models and authorities. But it is impossible to get much closer to them. The saga writers remain anonymous.

# 9 Icelanders—Nordic Storytellers and Bookworms

Stories have been told in all cultures and at all times, both about one's own experiences and those of others, as well as about contemporaneous and past events. In the Middle Ages, the Icelanders were famous for their historical knowledge and works. The Danish historian Saxo Grammaticus says in the preface to his *History of the Danes* from around 1200 that a large part of the work is based on Icelandic informants. He praises them for their historical diligence; according to Saxo, it is their pleasure to pass on "the history of all peoples." Later in his work, Saxo introduces a certain Icelander, Arnoldus Tylensis or Arnold the Icelander, who was a member of Bishop Absalon's retinue. Arnold was as good about predicting the future as he was knowledgeable about the past. According to Saxo, he was such a good storyteller that the Danish king once held him back against his will from one of Absalon's campaigns in order to listen to his stories. Obviously, it was not sagas of Icelanders which Arnold told the Danish king. Rather, the king probably wanted him to tell about the history of Denmark or other kingdoms. One can imagine that it was especially sagas of ancient times about Danish kings with which Arnold the Icelander entertained the king.

In a *þáttr* ("tale") about Sturla Þórðarson, who among other things was behind the aforementioned redaction of the *Book of Settlements*, there is a memorable account of an episode on board the ship of King Magnus Lawmender (1238–1280; reigned from 1263). *The Tale of Sturla* (*Sturlu þáttr*) has been transmitted in *The Saga of the Sturlungs* (*Sturlunga saga*), a collection of contemporary sagas:

> When everyone had gone to sleep, the king's forecastleman asked who would entertain with stories. Most of them remained silent. Then he said: "Sturla the Icelander, will you entertain?" "It's for you to decide," said Sturla. Then he told them the story of Huld better and more knowledgeably than any of those present had ever heard it before. Many of them gathered on the plankdeck, wanting to hear as clearly as possible. There was quite a crowd there. The queen asked: "What's that crowd of men on the deck?" A man replied: "These are men who

DOI: 10.4324/9781003499923-9

24    *The Sagas of Icelanders*

want to listen to the saga that the Icelander is telling." She asked: "What saga is that?" He answered: "It's about a great troll-woman, and it's a good saga, because it's being well told." The king asked her not to pay attention to this, but go to sleep. She said: "I think this Icelander is a man of honor and probably less worthy of disapproval than people say."

The next day Sturla is called before the king and queen to entertain them with the saga. The background for this story is that Sturla had to leave Iceland because of violent conflicts, in which he himself actively took part. The Norwegian King Magnus and his father, Haakon Haakonsson, are hostile to Sturla, because he has been slandered. But the *þáttr* tells how Sturla with his well-told saga quickly wins them over and at last with the help of his poems he achieves not only the favor of the king but also his friendship and trust. Consequently, he is assigned the honorable task of writing the biographies of the two kings, *Haakon's Saga* (*Hákonar saga Hákonarsonar*) and *Magnus Lawmender's Saga* (*Magnúss saga lagabœtir*). It was incredibly lucky for the king to meet such a talented historian as Sturla Þórðarson; without him, the history of the king would not have been documented. The *þáttr* demonstrates how composition and saga writing bring a brave and clever Icelander up and forward in the world. It emphasizes the value of literature. It could however be questioned whether King Haakon Haakonsson deserved a saga: He was the one responsible for the killing of Sturla's uncle Snorri Sturluson.

One also encounters persons in the narratives of the sagas and *þættir* ("tales") of Icelanders who relate historical narratives. In *The Saga of the Sworn Brothers*, Thorgrim tells in an apparently entertaining manner about his killing of Thorgeir, Thormod's sworn brother:

> At that moment, Egil came running into the booth and said, "You're too far away here. There's some excellent entertainment going on." Thormod asked, "Where have you come from? And what entertainment are you talking about?" Egil answered, "I was at Thorgrim Einarsson's booth. That's where most of the others at the assembly are too." Thormod said, "And what kind of entertainment is taking place there?" Egil said, "Thorgrim's telling a story." Thormod said, "This story he's telling, who is it about?" Egil answered, "I couldn't tell you who it's about, but I can tell you one thing—he certainly knows how to tell a good, entertaining tale. He's sitting on a chair outside his booth and people are sitting all around, listening to him." Thormod said: "Surely you can name someone in the story, especially since you say it's so enjoyable." Egil said, "There's a man called Thorgeir in the story, a great warrior. And it seemed to me that Thorgrim himself was in it quite a lot and did quite a bit of the attacking, as you might imagine. I wish you'd go over there and listen to the entertainment." "Perhaps I shall," said Thormod.
>
> (Chapter 23)

Thormod goes over to listen to the story, but it will not be anticipated here how the tale about the storytelling killer ends. In *The Tale of the Story-Wise Icelander* (*Íslendings þáttr sǫgufróða*), which is preserved in a manuscript from the middle of the thirteenth century, one meets an Icelander, who does not tell about his own exploits, but about the Norwegian king with whom he is staying. The Icelander gets to remain at court because he can tell stories. In fact, he is obliged to entertain the king's men whenever he is asked to. Eventually, however, the Icelander runs out of stories, and he becomes concerned, because the only story he has left is the tale about the king's own journey abroad. But this particular story is the one the king is most interested in hearing, and when the king has listened to this saga from beginning to end and approved of it, he asks the Icelander where he learned it. The Icelander replies that he learned parts of it every summer at the Althing in Iceland from Halldor, Snorri the Godi's son. In addition to the fact that the *þáttr*—like *The Saga of the Sworn Brothers*—mentions storytelling as entertainment, it also shows that in the thirteenth-century stories were learned by heart so that one could tell them in public. It is more likely, however, that Sturla Þórðarson brought with him a manuscript containing the saga of the troll-woman Huld, for the *þáttr* reports that the queen asked him "to bring along the saga."

Even though oral traditions existed, the sagas of Icelanders cannot have grown directly out of these. One must consider that the orality found in the sagas is to a considerable extent an illusion—after all, the sagas are written texts. The illusion about the sagas' orality was originally nurtured by the fact that the sagas were read aloud. There is only one reference in the sagas of Icelanders to the reading of stories and sagas. In *The Saga of the People of Fljotsdal*, we are told that "an excellent farmer" reads stories:

> Hreidar sat reading an old story until past nightfall. Then he went out and fed his cattle.
>
> (Chapter 13)

Unfortunately, the saga does not mention the circumstances. He might have been reading the story out loud for his household, but it cannot be excluded that he read it for himself. For a modern reader it is tempting to see in Hreidar a true bookworm, for the saga also says that "Hreidar was a man who never stopped work until the early hours, and slept right through to midday" (Chapter 13). According to the saga, the episode took place in the Saga Age and before the introduction of Christianity—and, by extension, books—in Iceland. It is therefore clear that the passage has no historical validity as a statement about conditions in the Saga Age. However, it has validity about the time the sagas were written, the Icelandic High Middle Ages. The medieval saga writer has anachronistically imagined Hreidar reading a parchment manuscript in the late hours of the evening and night. The idea of a farmer with a passionate interest in literature was remarkably not strange to him.

# 10 The Historicity of the Sagas of Icelanders

When the sagas of Icelanders insist on being read as historical narratives, the question arises about the extent to which the narratives are in agreement with historical events. In most cases, the question cannot be answered. In many instances, there is a historical background for the events, but we do not know to which degree it agrees with the narrative in the saga. The sagas of Icelanders took place before literacy was established in Iceland and Scandinavia, and since these sagas deal primarily with conditions in Iceland, it is impossible to check their contents against European chronicles and annals. In contrast, it is possible to do this in respect to some sagas of ancient times, but the result each time is that the historical events have been so changed as to be unrecognizable; often only the heroes' names have been preserved. But most of the events in the sagas of Icelanders cannot be checked because there are no contemporary sources. The curious reader is left with silent archaeological excavations and later sources, such as the *Book of Settlements* and Ari the Learned's *Book of Icelanders*. Sometimes, the saga writers have expanded the information in the *Book of Settlements* and told a fictitious tale about imaginary descendants of historical settlers. However, on occasion archaeological finds have confirmed the stories.

One must assume that in most cases there are great differences between the potentially factual events and their description in the sagas because of the extent of time between the event and the saga. The saga writer wants to tell a good story and gives his material a literary form. Sometimes, several versions of the same narrative have been transmitted. In such instances, it is clear that they cannot all be correct and that at least in some of them changes have been made. An example can be seen in *Hen-Thorir's Saga* and Ari the Learned's *Book of Icelanders*. The *Book of Icelanders* relates that Hen-Thorir burned Thorkel Blund-Ketils-son in his house, and that Hen-Thorir was then outlawed and killed. However, *Hen-Thorir's Saga* reports that Blund-Ketil was burned in his house, and that Hen-Thorir was killed before he had received his sentence. Despite the differences, the report of this burning in the *Book of Icelanders* is a clear indication that the burning took place. But the differences between the two narratives show that

DOI: 10.4324/9781003499923-10

the details or the exact circumstances of the event are unknown. Nonetheless, the *Book of Icelanders* should without doubt be considered the better source for this story.

### Njal's Saga

Another example is found in the account of Gunnar's last battle in the *Book of Settlements* (Sturla's redaction) and *Njal's Saga*. The *Book of Settlements* reports that in addition to Gunnar an adult male was present at the farm, while *Njal's Saga* claims that Gunnar was the only male. The saga writer exaggerated the tragic dimension in *Njal's Saga* by letting Gunnar fight alone. In the same way, the *Book of Settlements* reports that in a fight Gunnar kills four men, whereas *Njal's Saga* states that in the same fight he killed fourteen men. Once again, the saga has embellished the story. The saga writer sought to create a compelling story. This should perhaps not be surprising when the same saga says about Gunnar that he "could jump higher than his own height, in full fighting gear, and just as far backward as forward" (Chapter 19). One should bear in mind that full fighting gear is extremely heavy.

It is possible to compare certain sagas with foreign sources. That is the case with the account of the battle of Clontaf, which took place on Good Friday, April 23, 1014, in *Njal's Saga* and *Thorstein Sidu-Hallsson's Saga*. The battle was between Munster, under the leadership of King Brian Boru and Leinster, who had the support of the Scandinavians. Although King Brian was killed in the battle, Munster was victorious, while the other faction, which included the Vikings, suffered significant losses. Scholars have compared the Irish transmission of the Battle of Clontarf with the Icelandic depiction in *Njal's Saga*, and their investigations have revealed that although some details have been preserved in the Icelandic version, much has been changed. The historical events were given a literary form, in which the saga writer demonstrates greater interest in the individual than in foreign policy.

The burning of Njal's farm is also mentioned in texts older than *Njal's Saga*, so the event might well be historical. The burning is mentioned in annals (most of which date it to 1010) and in the *Book of Settlements*, which relates that Njal was burned in his house along with seven men at Bergthorshvol. The battle at the Althing is also mentioned in annals. In Snorri's *Edda* Burnt-Njal is mentioned, and in the kings' sagas, *The Saga of the Conversion* (*Kristni saga*) and in other works, the leader of the attack, Burning (*Brennu*)-Flosi, is given a nickname associated with burning. Indeed, the time of the burning has been estimated. According to most manuscripts containing *Njal's Saga*, the burning took place eight weeks before winter, that is, the night between August 21 and 22, 1010. However, archaeological finds at Bergþórshvoll have not revealed evidence of a fire in the living quarters; only the barn, shed, and stable show signs of burning. The Icelandic scholar Einar Ól. Sveinsson, who published his edition of the

28    *The Sagas of Icelanders*

saga in 1954 (in Íslenzk fornrit 12), believed that this was because people had carefully removed ashes and traces of the fire to construct a new building in the same place. Einar Ól. Sveinsson also concluded that the saga writer must have had access to certain pieces of information about the burning and the fight at the Althing. However, what was lacking in his sources, he added himself, enriching the saga with lively and detailed narratives. Recently, the Icelandic author Einar Kárason argued that the burning in the saga reflects a terrible event during the saga writer's own time, namely the burning at Flugumýri in 1253, where twenty-five persons were burned inside. A daughter of the aforementioned Sturla Þórðarson was present at Flugumýri, but she was rescued from the fire. In this manner, the saga writer may have incorporated contemporary events into the Saga Age narrative. Sturla Þórðarson was an especially active literary figure in thirteenth-century Iceland. Among other works, he wrote the contemporary *Saga of Icelanders* (*Íslendinga saga*), which recounts the burning at Flugumýri. Like *Njal's Saga*, *The Saga of Icelanders* is also divided into three parts, and, according to Einar Kárason, it is likely that Sturla Þórðarson is the writer of *Njal's Saga*. However, we will never receive a definitive answer on the matter.

### The Sagas about the Norse Discovery of America

In the 1960s, a sensational discovery emerged supporting the accounts in the sagas regarding the Norsemen's discovery of North America. The story of the Norsemen's expeditions is found in *The Saga of the Greenlanders* and *Eirik the Red's Saga*, both of which have been dated to the early thirteenth century. *The Saga of the Greenlanders*, the older of the two, comprises a number of *þættir* ("tales"), which are amalgamated into a saga, whereas *Eirik the Red's Saga*, which is based on *The Saga of the Greenlanders*, appears to a greater extent as a literary composition. *The Saga of the Greenlanders*, considered the most significant source about the Norsemen's voyages to North America, describes no fewer than seven expeditions to an unknown world. In *Eirik the Red's Saga*, the number of voyages and their outcome differ, and there is an increase in heathen and Christian elements compared to *The Saga of the Greenlanders*.

In *The Saga of the Greenlanders*, Eirik the Red is the first to settle in Greenland. His journey is followed by that of the Icelander Bjarni (a descendant of the famous settler Ingolf), but he drifts off course. He and his men lose their way, drift west of Greenland, and accidentally sail past three lands: a flat land covered by rocks, a forested land, and a mountainous island. When they finally reach Greenland, they are criticized for not having explored the unknown places they discovered. The following summer, Leif the Lucky sets off on the same course as Bjarni with a crew of thirty-five men. They find and name all the lands, which Bjarni passed by. They name the land, which looks like a large, flat rock covered with glaciers, Helluland ("Flat-stone land"), and the land covered by forests Markland ("Forest land"). The third and last land, which they explore, is rich in vegetation and animal life, and among other things they find grapes here, which is why Leif names the place Vinland ("Land of grapes"). The men then sail back to Greenland.

A number of other expeditions to this newly discovered land follow, but they are not as successful as Leif the Lucky's voyage. The next expedition perishes on the journey. When it is finally possible to reach the new land again, the Norsemen face natives (in Old Norse/Icelandic sources referred to as *skræling-jar*), and the two peoples come into conflict. The last voyage, however, is the worst. The travelers are now led by Eirik the Red's daughter, Freydis. She and her crew plan to settle permanently in Vinland, but the enterprise ends in catastrophe and savagery.

For a long time, scholars considered the two sagas pure fabrication, but in 1961 the Norwegian explorer Helge Ingstad and the archaeologist Anne Stine Ingstad found remains of Viking habitation at L'Anse aux Meadows in Newfoundland, Canada. Several dwellings, a smithy, and hearths were discovered, similar to those found in the Viking settlements in Greenland. The finds also included a spindle whorl identical to one found in Greenland. Carbon-14 analyses from the settlement, which showed no indication of having been inhabited for more than a few years, were dated to around 1000, aligning with the saga. Most people now concur that Helluland is probably the southern part of Baffin Island, and that Markland is the coast of Labrador or the northern part of Newfoundland. *The Saga of the Greenlanders*—and also *Eirik the Red's Saga*—preserve the memories of actual expeditions to North America. However, the details in the sagas, the fateful consequences of the journeys, and the perils of paganism in an unknown region must all be attributed to the saga writer.

### The Saga as a Reflection of Contemporary Times

It is tempting to believe that the sagas of Icelanders are based on historical events. But it is reasonable to assume that in most instances the historical core has been altered to such an extent that it is now unrecognizable—similar to Homer's account of the Trojan War, and the narratives about Jesus in the Bible. The interpretation of the burning in *Njal's Saga* as a reflection of contemporary events reveals that the sagas can be read as sources of the history of mentalities in a saga writer's own time.

Many of the sagas of Icelanders were written during the Sturlung Age in the thirteenth century, a tumultuous period marked by civil strife. This era culminated in the loss of Icelanders' independence and the incorporation of Iceland into the Norwegian realm. It is quite plausible that several of the sagas reflect contemporary debates for or against the Norwegian throne. Some sagas relate how the Icelandic hero thrives in the strictly hierarchical society of the Norwegian king, where he soon achieves honor and dignity. But when he returns to the horizontal social structure of Iceland, he is being fought by his neighbor farmers and eventually succumbs.

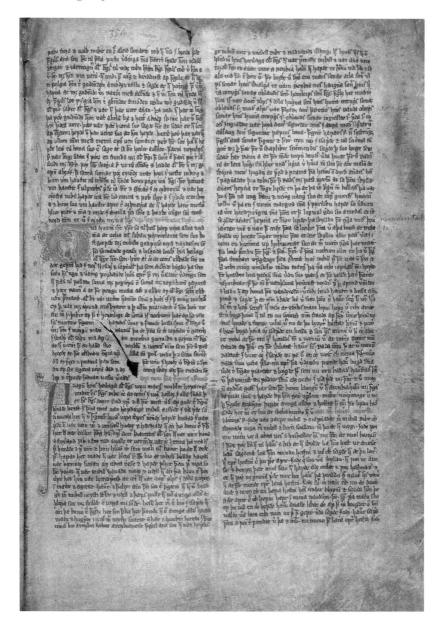

*Figure 10.1* The Saga of the Sworn Brothers begins in the manuscript Flateyjarbók with a unique introduction, which explains how the saga should be interpreted. GKS 1005 fol. (ca. 1387–1395), Árni Magnússon Institute for Icelandic Studies, Reykjavík. Photo: Jóhanna Ólafsdóttir.

*The Historicity of the Sagas of Icelanders*   31

This is the case in *The Saga of Finnbogi the Mighty* and *The Saga of Bjorn, Champion of the Hitardal People*. Generally, the saga is structured in such a way that in the first part the hero matures and thrives at the court of the Norwegian king, and thereafter he returns home to Iceland, where almost everything goes wrong. In *The Saga of the Sworn Brothers*, however, this structure is reversed. Thorgeir, one of the two sworn brothers, is an unruly and violent man. In the horizontal social structure of Iceland, no one can control him; he kills a shepherd for no other reason than that "he stood so well poised for a blow" (Flateyjarbók-redaction, Chapter 8), and he even wants to measure himself against his sworn brother Thormod. Eventually, he is outlawed, which is reasonable, for he poses a danger to others wherever he is. But when he becomes a member of the retinue of King Olaf the Saint things change—because, as is written in the introduction to the saga in Flateyjarbók, the king can control him:

> It is a sign of King Olaf's power and luck that he could control such great troublemakers as these sworn brothers to such an extent that they loved the king above all others. All their deeds, which they performed in honor of the king, also gave them fame and a good reputation, and with courage and manliness they put up a superb resistance before they ended their life and accomplishments in this miserable world.
>
> (Flateyjarbók-redaction, Chapter 1)

Other sagas, however, express a clear resistance to Norwegian royal power. They show how the hero is destroyed by the king but remains peaceful and thrives upon returning to the free society in Iceland. The best example is *Egil's Saga*. Egil's family personifies the two attitudes toward Norwegian royal power. The family is divided into two branches of people: the beautiful and fair, and the dark and ugly. The beautiful and fair are credulous and loyal vis-à-vis royal power, but they are destroyed by it. The dark and ugly are suspicious, independent, and contrary vis-à-vis royal power—and they survive. It is, of course, the latter group to which Egil belongs, and he especially has a strained relationship with Norwegian royal power, especially Eirik Blood-axe and his queen Gunnhild. While in Norway, Egil commits outrageous acts: He pricks out the eye of a man, tears the throat of another man with his teeth, and deliberately vomits profusely over a third. His overweening confidence vis-à-vis royal power is so great that he kills the young son of King Eirik and Queen Gunnhild and erects a scorn pole directed against them. Egil's scorn pole consists of the severed head of a horse on a hazel pole, which, through sorcery, is intended to expel Eirik Blood-axe and Gunnhild from Norway. According to the saga's logic, it is precisely because of the scorn pole that the royal couple is forced to leave Norway. During his adult life in Iceland, however, he is a peaceful man.

# 11  Style and Literary Technique

In contrast to the sagas of ancient times (*fornaldarsögur*), the sagas of Icelanders are often singled out as factual narratives devoid of exaggerations or fantastical or paranormal elements. The word "realism" has often been used to describe the sagas of Icelanders, but for medieval literature, this term is anachronistic. Many episodes in the sagas of Icelanders are fantastic—or at least appear to be historically untrustworthy to a modern reader. In many sagas, there are people skilled in magic, who, by means of *seiðr* (a form of sorcery), cause the death and ill fortune of others. In *Njal's Saga* the phenomenon "blood-rain" occurs; Gunnar's spear suddenly becomes bloody, which forebodes the ensuing battle. In the same saga, a series of curious events occurs at the same time as the Battle of Clontarf: A man in Ireland sees some women using human heads instead of weight looms, human intestines instead of wefts and warps, a sword instead of a weaver's reed and an arrow instead of a weaver's rod, and at Svinafell in Iceland blood drips on a priest's chasuble. Dangerous revenants and mound-dwellers appear, for example, in *The Saga of the People of Eyri*, *The Saga of the People of Svarfadardal*, *The Saga of Grettir the Strong*, *The Saga of Hord and the People of Holm*, and *Bard's Saga*. In *Njal's Saga*, Gunnar's burial mound opens up, where Gunnar sits "happy" and with a "very cheerful look," while reciting a verse and looking at the moon (Chapter 78). In *The Saga of the People of Vatnsdal*, an amulet magically appears in Iceland to indicate where an immigrant is fated to settle. One meets animals, which are supernatural or are accomplices of demonic powers; examples are found in *The Saga of the People of Eyri*, *The Saga of the People of Laxardal*, and *The Saga of the People of Floi*. In *The Saga of the People of Eyri*, mysterious and sinister events take place on the farm Froda; these are the so-called "Fróðá-wonders." First a half-moon appears on the wall, a weird-moon, which forebodes death, and after that the place is plagued by death and misery. A drowned and soaked ship's crew enters and sits down by the fire night after night, joined by the buried dead who are fouled with soil. The haunting does not end until a priest holds a trial and passes sentence on the dead. For the modern reader, such elements suggest that the sagas are not historical. But for a reader or listener in the Middle Ages, these elements were part of reality as they imagined it.

DOI: 10.4324/9781003499923-11

*Style and Literary Technique*   33

A number of elements occur in various sagas of Icelanders; they are literary topoi or clichés: The Icelandic hero soon becomes the king's confidant. Two brothers are the opposite of each other in both appearance and temperament. A horse-fight leads to conflict. A skald has a problematic mindset. A slave has a nasty character. The marriage of a woman from a distinguished family and a man from an inferior family turns out badly. A man insists on taking off alone exactly when his enemies lie in wait for him. A young man is a so-called coal-biter, a good-for-nothing, who lies around by the fire and is an embarrassment to his family, but who eventually gets up from the kitchen floor and proves his worth.

The plot is often foreshadowed by prophetic dreams, predictions, or omens. This gives the sagas a fatalistic tinge. Early on in *The Saga of the People of Laxardal*, Gudrun worries about her dreams. The dreams are interpreted by one of her relatives, and the interpretation serves as both a brief summary of her future marriages and the fates of her husbands (Chapter 33). In *The Saga of Droplaug's Sons*, Helgi dreams that he and his men will be attacked, and his own chin and set of teeth split apart, which indeed happens the following day (Chapter 10). The dreams' predictions of events show that fate has been decided and cannot be altered. However, what captivates the reader is likely not the outcome but rather the manner in which the individual in the saga confronts his or her fate.

One learns several times in *Gisli Sursson's Saga* that fortune does not favor Gisli. Good fortune does not necessarily smile upon a good and honorable person. The deterministic view of humankind in the sagas is powerfully expressed in *Gisli Sursson's Saga* through an image of rivers flowing in a certain direction: "Now all the waters flow toward Dyrafjord," says Vestein, realizing that his life is in imminent danger if he continues to Dyrafjord, but he must nevertheless go (Chapter 12). Human beings cannot stop the flow of water nor alter fate.

A particular characteristic of the sagas of Icelanders is their objective representation. Unlike the photography-inspired narrative style of the nineteenth century, they lack long, panoramic descriptions of the land, farms, or people. Nor are there in the sagas any poetically or epically formulaic comparisons, as in Homer, or detailed discussions of moral topics or the nature of women as in Saxo's *History of the Danes*. Only rarely does the saga writer insert a learned precept. *The Saga of the Sworn Brothers* in Flateyjarbók is unique with its learned digressions, and *Viglund's Saga* is exceptional in the sense that it provides a short passage on the nature of love:

> Viglund and Ketilrid loved each other even more ardently now than they had while growing up. They had such a secret love concealed in their hearts that their deeply entrenched love and the fruit of their affection could never be uprooted from their hearts, since this is the nature of true love. For the fire of affection and the flames of love burn all the more intensely, and weld together the hearts and minds of lovers all the more tightly, the greater the number of

34    *The Sagas of Icelanders*

those who wish to injure them and the greater the obstacles that families place in the path of those whom love and affection have brought together, as was the case with these two, Viglund and Ketilrid.

(Chapter 12)

Conversely, the learned passages in *The Saga of the Sworn Brothers* have a more theological character and express a particular interest in the anatomy of courage:

Everyone who heard these tidings thought it remarkable that one young man on his own should have slain such an experienced fighter and chieftain as Jod. And yet it was no great wonder since the Almighty Creator had forged in Thorgeir's breast such a strong and sturdy heart that he was as fearless and brave as a lion in whatever trials or tribulations befell him. And as all good things come from God, so too does steadfastness, and it is given unto all bold men together with a free will that they may themselves choose whether they do good or evil. Thus Jesus Christ has made Christians his sons and not his slaves, so that he might reward all according to their deeds.

(Chapter 3)

The learned passages in the Flateyjarbók version of *The Saga of the Sworn Brothers* have been used as an argument that this redaction of the saga is not the oldest. Incidentally, in the same redaction of *The Saga of the Sworn Brothers* epic comparisons reminiscent of Homer have been added, a feature not otherwise found in the sagas. It is said that it is more dangerous to attack Thorgeir than "a lioness, when the cubs are taken away from her, and by nature she is the fiercest" (Flateyjarbók-redaction, Chapter 24). But such examples are extremely rare. They are not considered to be typical saga style but rather signs of influence from European literature. It is possible that they belong to the oldest period of saga writing, as similar theological considerations are found in the oldest saga, Oddr Snorrason's *Saga of Olaf Tryggvason* from the latter half of the twelfth century. Snorri Sturluson used this saga in *Heimskringla*, where he deleted the theological exegeses, which resulted in his famous saga style.

However, it is not that the Icelandic saga writers did not aim to educate the reader about important truths, such as the infidelity of women and the cowardice of enslaved people. It is just that they simply chose to convey these verities through examples and stories. It may be that they did not feel they had the authority to educate and to pass judgment in this manner. The saga writers, who preserve their anonymity, never mention their patrons—unlike, for example, Geoffrey of Monmouth who refers to the archbishop of Oxford.

The narrator of the sagas of Icelanders rarely steps forward, and it is even more rare for him to pass judgment on events in the sagas. Instead, he uses stereotypical phrases, such as "people say" (*menn segja*), "it is told" (*þat er sagt*), and "now it is to be told of" (*nú er at segja frá, nú er þar til at taka*).

As mentioned above, these expressions have contributed to the perception of the sagas as oral narratives, as they give the impression that the saga writer is simply a mediator of an existing tradition. Yet, these phrases are also used indirectly to conceal the attitude of the narrator. They soon became a firm stylistic component of the sagas of Icelanders.

Quite often, the sagas are introduced by "I" or "we." *The Saga of the People of Vopnafjord* begins with the words: "We take up the thread of this story when a man named Helgi lived at Hof in Vopnafjord," and *The Saga of Finnbogi the Mighty* concludes with the words: "And there I conclude the saga of Finnbogi." The last line of *Njal's Saga* is: "And here I end the saga of the burning of Njal." *Bolli Bollason's tale*, which appears after *The Saga of the People of Laxardal* in the manuscript Möðruvallabók, ends with the words: "We have heard no more of the story than this." This is likely a comment by the redactor of the manuscript on the saga and the tale, as they have been transmitted in this manuscript. Sometimes, the narrator also peeks out, when there is a shift of scene: "Now we shall leave for a while the account of Thormod Kolbrun's Poet," *The Saga of the Sworn Brothers* says, when the narrator turns to a different topic (Chapter 11). On rare occasions, the narrator also lets his opinion shine through, as happens in *The Saga of Finnbogi the Mighty*: "And we assert that there have been few or none in Iceland mightier [than Finnbogi] among those not shape-shifters" (Chapter 36).

The language of the sagas of Icelanders often comes close to the spoken language. The sentences are typically short with coordinate clauses, and the vocabulary is simple. In a few sagas, there are touches of a learned or Latin style with longer sentences and more subordinate clauses, as in the above excerpt from *Viglund's Saga*. Litotes, a form of understatement through double negatives is a commonly used stylistic device. In *The Saga of the Sworn Brothers*, when it is said about Kolbrun that she was "not completely small," it implies that she was, in fact, large (Chapter 11; my translation). "Not few" is the same as many (*The Saga of the Sworn Brothers*, Chapter 4; my translation); and when someone is "not completely opposed," to something, he will do it (Chapter 3); and when Thorgeir comments that he "cannot deny [his] part" in a killing, then he is, of course, the killer (Chapter 3). Related to litotes is a type of understatement that also occurs in the tough hero's rejoinders. In the same chapter of the saga, when Thorgeir remarks that a wound "will not need binding" after having killed his father's killer, it becomes evident that he received not a small scratch but a deadly wound (Chapter 3). When his sworn brother Thormod is mortally wounded after the battle for Saint Olaf at Stiklestad, he also says: "The only wounds I have need no binding" (Flateyjarbók-redaction, Chapter 24).

The saga writers are often impressed by the strength of men from the past, a sentiment that is reflected in the above remarks; nonetheless, the sagas often problematize heroism. Along with understatements, superlatives are often used in the language of the sagas in descriptions of magnificent men or women.

36   *The Sagas of Icelanders*

The men's courage is often given expression in their laconic remarks, as yet another example from *The Saga of the Sworn Brothers* demonstrates. When Thorgeir and Thormod are picking angelica at Hornstrandir, Thorgeir suddenly disappears. What Thormod does not know is that Thorgeir is dangling from Hornbjarg, a famous crag about 400–500 meters high, and that he is only hanging onto a stalk of angelica. Thormod shouts to him:

> Thorgeir replied, his voice unwavering and no trace of fear in his heart.
> "I reckon," he said, "I'll have enough once I've uprooted this piece I'm holding."
>
> (Flateyjarbók-redaction, Chapter 13)

Thorgeir is as hard as a bone and so fearless that he would rather fall to his death than ask for help. Thormod knows the style and therefore understands that his sworn brother is in extreme danger of death and hurries to rescue him. It is a remarkable mixture of admiration and razor-sharp rejoinders—to us it is humorous, but it is hard to know, whether the saga writers and their primary public laughed in the same way and at the same passages as we do today.

Another example is found in *Njal's Saga*, when Gizur the White and his men turn up to kill Gunnar. A man climbs onto the roof of the house to see whether Gunnar is at home, but he is struck by Gunnar's halberd. Once back, the men ask whether Gunnar was there, and he replies: "Find that out for yourselves, but I've found out one thing—that his halberd's at home." Then he falls down dead (Chapter 77). The last words of Atli, Grettir's brother, are also of the same type. He is struck by a spear and before he collapses, he comments: "Broad spears are the fashion these days" (Chapter 45).

The staging is scenic and resembles a theatrical performance. It alternates between direct and indirect speech, often transitioning seamlessly. In some sagas, half the text consists of dialogue, often on a high level and with great psychological insight. Through dialogue and plot individuals are depicted. Sometimes, the style seems more adjusted and perhaps more archaic in the dialogue. One has the sense that the saga writer wanted to let the heroes of the past speak in a terse, wise, and effective manner. Occasionally the dialogue also has a proverbial character.

Generally, the narrator limits himself to describing external conditions and relates what can be seen; he does not pass on his insight into the psychology of the characters. He leaves the interpretation of the saga heroes' inner life to the reader. *Egil's Saga* does not relate that Egil is in love with his brother's widow. We only read that he goes aside and pulls the cloak up over his head (Chapter 56). Incidentally, Odysseus does the same out of grief in Homer's *Odyssey*. When Gudrun's prophetic dreams are interpreted in *The Saga of the People of Laxardal*, she turns "blood-red," and yet her following reply is completely calm and collected (Chapter 33). Nonetheless, the reader understands that she is very

*Style and Literary Technique* 37

agitated. When Flosi is forced against his will to take responsibility for avenging Hoskuld in *Njal's Saga* and eventually burns Njal and his household in their home, his face becomes "in turns as red as blood, as pale as grass, and as black as Hel itself" (Chapter 116). The reader has no doubt that he is very much opposed to the impending revenge. One also reads in the sagas about young men and women, who talk with each other for a long time. They only do this, when they are very much in love, but in every case this interpretation is left to the reader. If in contrast a hero turns silent, one knows that something is wrong. When the Icelandic hero at the Norwegian court suddenly becomes silent and stops participating in the merriment, it is a clear sign that he is homesick and soon wants to go back to Iceland.

On a few occasions, however, there is internal focalization that gives insight into the inner life of individuals and the readers learn what they think or believe in certain situations. An example is found in the scene of the famous killing in *Gisli Sursson's Saga*. One night, Gisli slipped into the dark house in order to kill his brother-in-law Thorgrim. Accidentally, he first touches his sister Thordis, and the saga relates that "She thought it had been [Thorgrim's] hand that touched her." When Gisli places his hand on his brother-in-law in order to wake him before the killing, the saga relates that "Thorgrim thought it is Thordis who roused him and he turned towards her" (Chapter 16). Later on in *Gisli Sursson's Saga*, there is a rare example of the narrator disclosing his opinion, when Gisli, in a poem, reveals that he has killed Thorgrim with words "which should not have been spoken" (Chapter 18), the narrator notes. In *The Saga of the People of Eyri*, the narrator knows what a slave is thinking: "Egil felt it would only be a little while before he earned for himself everlasting freedom" (Chapter 43). The slave has been promised his freedom, if he kills a man, but he trips on a loose tassel on his shoe and ends up losing his life. Typically, however, the narrator does not comment on the actions of people or deeds. This feature of saga style almost reminds one of Gustave Flaubert's 'absent narrator,' but the difference between the style of the sagas of the Icelanders and the French photo-realism of the nineteenth century is enormous. Accordingly, one cannot describe the style of the sagas by merely saying that the saga writer prefers to show rather than tell. It is more difficult than this to explain the style of the sagas. The narrative mode is primarily dramatic due to the many instances of dialogue. The psychological depth of individuals is created through their speeches and in dialogue.

Instead of passing his own judgment on the events, the narrator refers to people's attitudes ("it is believed," "people thought") or facts (a case is negatively commented on, an individual achieves honor from an action or event). Comments by public opinion may have an extradiegetic effect on a given saga's audience, but they also have an intradiegetic effect on the reputation, and there on the actions, of characters within the saga. In *The Saga of the People of Laxardal*, the narrator lets it suffice to refer to what "was obvious" and what "most people

38    *The Sagas of Icelanders*

assumed," after Gudrun Osvifsdottir found out that Bolli had lied about Kjartan in order to trick her into marrying him. The saga reports that:

> Although Gudrun hardly spoke of the matter, it was obvious that she was anything but happy, and most people assumed that she regretted having lost Kjartan, though she tried to conceal it.

(Chapter 44)

When Kjartan's father, Olaf Peacock, advises Bolli not to propose to Gudrun, he refers (like a saga narrator) to the fact that Bolli clearly knows "that the affection between Kjartan and Gudrun was spoken of everywhere" (Chapter 43). As a reader, one often clearly senses the saga writer's attitude toward events and heroes, even though it is not explicitly stated. This applies to saga heroes like Gunnar and Njal in *Njal's Saga* and Gisli in *Gisli Sursson's Saga*. But it is more difficult to figure out the saga writer's attitude toward more complicated individuals, such as Flosi in *Njal's Saga*, Egil, Killer-Glum, and Hrafnkel.

The sagas are not constructed according to the classic rules of narrative art. A saga never begins in medias res, and it does not meet the requirement of unity of plot. Before the action begins, the individuals are briefly and concisely presented. The typical introductory formula is: "A man was named …" / "There was a man named." Generally, information is provided about the individuals' family, home, physical appearance, temperament, skills, and, not least, position in society. In addition, the reader gets to know the characters through their actions and in conversations with others, but the introductory characterizations of persons can always be trusted. When an individual is described in an introductory characterization, it signals to the reader that this person is important to the plot of the saga. There is a tendency to not have individuals undergo any development during the course of the saga, though there are exceptions. In *The Saga of Hrafnkel Frey's Godi*, Hrafnkel discontinues his worship of Frey. In his saga, Gisli becomes gentler and milder toward people of humble means during his outlawry. The roughneck Grettir becomes afraid of the dark after his struggle with the revenant Glam. And the formerly strong Egil grows old; he eventually stumbles around by the fire and becomes a nuisance to the servants.

The narrative shifts between detailed descriptions of, for example, fights or intrigues and brief statements that now the winter passed without noteworthy events. The latter concludes or introduces the chapters. Descriptions of nature are rare in the sagas of Icelanders, even though the Icelandic landscape with its gorges, passes, and mountain heaths is constantly present. As a reader, one continuously follows in the footsteps of the saga heroes. An example is found in *The Saga of Hrafnkel Frey's Godi*, when the narrator reduces the tempo of the narrative in the scene which describes Hrafnkel pursuit of Sam's brother. Suddenly, the narrator dwells on the landscape, the difficult moors, and in this way prolongs the scene, whereby he creates intolerable suspense before the killing.

*Style and Literary Technique*   39

Typically, descriptions of nature appear only to the extent that they are of importance to the plot. Gunnar's famous comment on the beauty of the land in *Njal's Saga* is unique:

> Gunnar happened to face the hillside and the farm at Hlidarendi and said: "So lovely is the hillside that it has never before seemed to me as lovely as now, with its pale fields and mown meadows; and I'll ride back home and not go anywhere at all."

(Chapter 75)

It is worth noting that here Gunnar is referring to the fertile farmland and not the majestic landscape. Between us and the saga writers is pre-Romanticism and the veneration of the wild landscape in Romanticism.

Despite the many similarities outlined in this chapter, it must be emphasized that the individual sagas of Icelanders exhibit great differences in style, structure, and theme. They were written over a long period of time and by different authors with different tastes and preferences; some saga writers have a penchant for tragic narratives, while in the second creative flowering of saga writing in the late Middle Ages there seems to be more inclination toward humor.

# 12 Skaldic Poetry

In addition to the many instances of speech mentioned above, poems also function as dramatic lines in the sagas. The stanzas in the sagas of Icelanders are skaldic verse, though some of them contain eddic poetry or mixtures of the two modes (like Egil's *Loss of Sons*). Saga heroes are most often silent about their inner life in their rejoinders, but feelings can be expressed in poetry. A subgroup of the sagas of Icelanders, skalds' sagas, have skalds as their protagonist. They comprise *Kormak's saga*, *The Saga of Hallfred the Troublesome Poet*, *The Saga of Gunnlaug Serpent-Tongue*, and *The Saga of Bjorn, Champion of the Hitardal People*. *Egil's Saga* and *The Saga of the Sworn Brothers* also belong to this group, although only peripherally. The skalds are often complicated individuals; they fall madly in love, have an impetuous temperament, and do not hide their light under a bushel. In comparison, Thorgeir, who never recites a single verse, is characterized in *The Saga of the Sworn Brothers* as follows: "It is said that Thorgeir was not much of a ladies' man. He said it was demeaning to his strength to stoop to women" (Chapter 3). Notably, he does not share his concern about the mollifying effect of love with the skalds.

The skaldic poems have a high status in the society of the sagas. The most distinguished form of skaldic poetry is the *drápa*, which is a poem in honor of someone, often with a refrain (*stef*). A *flokkr*, which is a panegyric without a refrain, is less distinguished than a *drápa*. With a panegyric of high quality, the saga hero can quickly gain access to a king's or an earl's inner circle. This is evident in *The Saga of Gunnlaug Serpent-Tongue*, where the teenager skald more or less goes on tour from country to country. In England, Gunnlaug recites a poem "expressively and confidently," and the king gives him as a reward:

> a cloak of scarlet lined with the finest furs and with an embroidered band stretching down to the hem. He also made him one of his followers.
>
> (Chapter 7)

In Ireland, he subsequently recites a *drápa* and now receives a "new suit of scarlet clothes, an embroidered tunic, a cloak lined with exquisite furs and a gold

*Skaldic Poetry* 41

bracelet which weighed a mark" (Chapter 8). On the Orkney Islands, he recites a *flokkr*, which is "well-constructed" and receives as payment "a broad axe, decorated all over with silver inlay" along with the offer to stay with the earl and his retinue (Chapter 8). The journey continues to Västergötland, Sweden, where Gunnlaug recites a *flokkr* before the earl, who as thanks invites him to stay for the winter. After that, Gunnlaug travels to the king in Uppsala, where he quarrels with his countryman Hrafn about who should be the first to recite a poem before the king, whereafter he cuts Hrafn down to size before the king. Incidentally, this is where the deadly conflict between Gunnlaug and Hrafn begins. A skaldic poem revealing a poet's talent is cultural capital, which can easily be exchanged for wealth, power, and social prestige. There is a lot at stake when the skalds recite their poems.

Sometimes, the skalds and saga heroes recite single verses; these verses are called "loose verses" (*lausavísur*) and do not have the same status as poems. These situational verses are often recited on the spot as a comment on a particular situation, and sometimes they provide insight into the emotional life of the skald. In contrast to the emotionally reserved and detached comments in direct speech, the saga heroes can express their feelings in the artistic language of the poems. Longer poems demand a poet's preparation, and in the sagas, they are to a higher degree presented as professional work.

Now and then, however, more is at stake than wealth and power. In *Egil's Saga*, poetry is several times a matter of life and death. Because of Queen Gunnhild's witchcraft, Egil ends up against his will in the arms of his deadly enemy Eirik Blood-axe, who is residing in York. Egil has killed the royal couple's young son, but thanks to the intervention of his friend Arinbjorn, Egil manages to save his life by composing a poem in honor of the king. In the course of one night, he composes *Head Ransom*, which he recites the following day before the angry gaze of the king, and as a reward Egil receives his own ugly head. Some scholars are of the opinion that in this coerced poem of praise in honor of his deadly enemy, Egil maintains an ironic distance in the poetic circumlocutions. Egil's great art consists in the fact that on the surface the poem is a panegyric, whereas in reality it is an expression of contempt.

When, later in the saga, Egil's favorite son Bodvar drowns, Egil lies down in his bed-closet, wanting to die from sorrow. Egil's wife asks their daughter Thorgerd for help. Thorgerd cleverly coaxes her father to regain his spirit by appealing to his poetic talent and pride:

> Thorgerd replied in a loud voice, "I have had no evening meal, nor shall I do so until I go to join Freyja. I know no better course of action than my father's. I do not want to live after my father and brother are dead." She went to the door to Egil's bed-closet and called out, "Father, open the door, I want both of us to go the same way." Egil unfastened the door. Thorgerd walked in to the bed-closet and closed the door again. Then she lay down in

42   *The Sagas of Icelanders*

another bed that was there. Then Egil said, "You do well, my daughter, in wanting to follow your father. You have shown great love for me. How can I be expected to want to live with such great sorrow?" Then they were silent for a while. Then Egil said, "What are you doing, my daughter? Are you chewing something?" "I'm chewing dulse," she replied, "because I think it will make me feel worse. Otherwise I expect I shall live too long." "Is it bad for you?" asked Egil. "Very bad," said Thorgerd. "Do you want some?" "What difference does it make?" he said. A little later she called out for something to drink, and she was brought some water. Then Egil said, "That happens if you eat dulse, it makes you even thirstier." "Would you like a drink, father?" she asked. She passed him the animal horn and he took a great draught. Then Thorgerd said, "We've been tricked. This is milk." Egil bit a lump from the horn, as much as he could get his teeth into, then threw the horn away. Then Thorgerd said, "What shall we do now? Our plan has failed. Now I want us to stay alive, father, long enough for you to compose a poem in Bodvar's memory and I shall carve it onto a rune-stick. Then we can die if we want to. I doubt whether your son Thorstein would ever compose a poem for Bodvar, and it is unseemly if his memory is not honoured, because I do not expect us to be sitting there at the feast when it is." Egil said it was unlikely that he would be able to compose a poem even if he attempted to. "But I shall try," he said.

(Chapter 79)

Egil then composes *Loss of Sons* about his sorrow and anger at Odin, who gave him the gift of poetry but took his sons. This deeply personal poem is his way back to life, making it sensationally modern.

**The Poetic Language**

Skaldic poems are artistic verses that, in terms of syntax and vocabulary, are far removed from common prose language. The skalds use specific poetic words (Icelandic *heiti*) not found in prose, and use poetic circumlocutions, so-called kennings (Icelandic singular *kenning*, plural *kenningar*), which consist of at least two elements, at most seven. A simple kenning may be a "breaker of rings" (a generous man) or a "horse of the sail" (a ship). The "breaker of rings of the horse of the sail" is a man. But the kennings are often more complicated and are frequently based on myths and stories about the gods. A kenning for gold can be "Kraki's seeds," because Hrolf Kraki scattered gold on the field to stop the pursuing Swedes. "The destroyer of Kraki's seeds" can be used as a kenning for man. The skalds devise kennings for a number of concepts, in particular: warrior, woman, gold, ship, battle, sword, shield, and raven. A warrior can be paraphrased as "the tree of the sword;" a sword can again be paraphrased as "the flame of the battle;" and finally a battle can be paraphrased as "Odin's game," whereby one has a kenning consisting of four links. "Odin's game's flame of battle's tree" = man. Or "Odin's game's wrestler of Kraki's seeds," which also means man.

Even though kennings may often appear somewhat stereotypical, they are not empty of content. In a number of verses in *The Saga of Hallfred the Troublesome Poet*, the skald Hallfred comments on the use of heathen kennings. Hallfred has just been baptized by the Norwegian missionary king, Olaf Tryggvason, where-after he composes some stanzas about his loss of paganism and his problem as a Christian of not being able to use heathen kennings in his poetry. In his verses Hallfred presents paganism with a mixture of nostalgia and rejection. His verses address the fact that he can no longer sacrifice to the heathen gods and how, in earlier times, the skalds adapted their poems in order to gain Odin's favor. In his verses, the skald gives poetic expression to his personal reckoning with hea-then belief; in his view the kennings based on heathen myths belong to the old world, which he has left with his conversion. Other skalds, however, integrated the heathen kennings and adapted them to Christianity. In a poem in honor of the Christian saint Placid, *Plácitusdrápa*, composed in the twelfth century, the anonymous poet uses some of Odin's many names as a baseword in kennings for Placid, among others "fire-Thrott [= Odin] of the assembly of spears" = war-rior (stanza 48). And in a Christian poem by Einar Gilsson composed in the fourteenth century in honor of Bishop Guðmundur Arason yet another name for Odin appears in a kenning for the archbishop himself: "the wine's stronghold's [chalice] arch-Thund [name for Odin]" = archbishop (stanza 12).

The word order of the skaldic poems is completely free, which is possible because Old Norse/Icelandic is an inflected language. The splintered syntax can-not be reproduced in English translations. Most of the verses are in the so-called *dróttkvætt* ("court poetry") meter. A *dróttkvætt* verse consists of eight lines, two half-verses, each of four lines. The lines have six syllables. The lines are recip-rocally linked and constructed on the basis of an ingenious system of rhyme, alliteration, and stress. Other verses have a simpler structure, and this applies to Egil's three great poems: *Head Ransom*, *Loss of Sons*, and *Arinbjorn's Poem* (*Arinbjarnarkviða*); these are all composed using the metrical form *kviðuháttr* (literally "song-meter"), which is an offshoot from the less intricate meters of the eddic poems.

# 13 The Society of the Sagas of Icelanders

The plot of most of the sagas of Icelanders takes place in the period following the Age of Settlement, ca. 930–1030. Iceland was settled primarily from Norway, but people immigrated also from other places such as Ireland. The settlement was documented already in the twelfth century in the aforementioned *Book of Settlements*. Some of the settlers did not travel directly to Iceland, but stayed first in Scotland, on the Orkney Islands, the Shetland Islands, or the Hebrides, as related in *The Saga of the People of Laxardal* and *The Saga of the People of Kjalarnes*. The *Book of Settlements* mentions roughly 430 farmers and the areas which they settled. Around 1100, there were, according to the *Book of Icelanders*, around 4500 landowners. The first settlers took large tracts of land into possession, which they later divided among family members and friends.

**Belief and Religion**

With the immigration of people from Celtic regions, Christianity was introduced already during the Age of Settlement, even though Christianity was not accepted as the official and universal religion at the Althing until 1000. When the sagas were recorded, everyone in Iceland had already long been good Christians. The saga writers composed their stories with a Christian glance back to the transition from the old to the new faith. One can read in *The Saga of the People of Laxardal* and *The Saga of the People of Kjalarnes* about Christian pioneers (Unn the Deep-minded and Esja), but most of the immigrants were heathens. Even though some of the settlers were Christians, the official introduction of Christianity was an epoch-making event. It plays a significant role in *Njal's Saga*. In *The Saga of the People of Laxardal*, people travel from afar to see the piously fasting Kjartan (Chapter 45), but a Christian tone is also evident in *The Saga of the People of Vopnafjord*, *The Saga of the People of Kjalarnes*, and *The Saga of the People of Vatnsdal*. Several sagas contain dramatic descriptions of the religious merging of cultures: In *The Saga of the People of Fljotsdal*, Helgi destroys a heathen temple (Chapter 26). Bui does the same in *The Saga of the People of Kjalarnes*, and for this reason he is sentenced to outlawry and pursued (Chapter 4).

DOI: 10.4324/9781003499923-13

The Society of the Sagas of Icelanders   45

In *The Saga of the People of Floi*, a Christian and a heathen family undertake an ill-fated journey to Greenland. The troubles are due to the fact that, shortly before the departure, Thorgils was baptized; now the god Thor wants revenge. Their misfortunes begin on the voyage; they drift around on the sea, and it turns out that this is because they have an ox on board, which was once dedicated to Thor. They throw the ox overboard and only narrowly reach their destination. In Greenland, the heathen family dies and shows up as revenants, whereas a small group of the Christians survives but are pursued and tormented by an evil spirit in the form of a bird, who tempts the men to transgress the norms, among other things by drinking their own urine because of thirst. But Thorgils, the protagonist of the saga, intervenes, and because of him they receive help from God, and the demon leaves them. The saga reports that Thorgils is the ancestor of Thorlak (1133–1193), Iceland's saint.

Only few individuals in the sagas of Icelanders worship the heathen gods, and those who practice sorcery are most often the enemies of the heroes; a family from the Hebrides in *The Saga of the People of Laxardal*, with their *seiðr* (a form of sorcery), causes the death of Gudrun's second husband (Chapter 35) and later also of Hrut's son (Chapter 37). A few sagas describe heathen cults; in *The Saga of the People of Eyri*, the settler Thorolf Moster-beard builds a large temple dedicated to Thor:

> Beyond that point, the temple was a sanctuary. At the inner end there was a structure similar to the choir in churches nowadays and there was a raised platform in the middle of the floor like an altar, where a ring weighing twenty *ounces* and fashioned without a join was placed, and all oaths had to be sworn on this ring. It also had to be worn by the temple priest at all public gatherings. A sacrificial bowl was placed on the platform and in it a sacrificial twig—like a priest's aspergillum—was used to sprinkle blood from the bowl. This blood, which was called sacrificial blood, was the blood of live animals offered to the gods. The gods were placed around the platform in the choir-like structure within the temple.
>
> (Chapter 4)

For a long time, it was believed that the description of the heathen temple was authentic, but scholars now agree that it is a product of the medieval imagination. The saga writers' Christian attitude toward heathen matters is also reflected throughout the saga. Archaeologists have never found a heathen temple in Scandinavia or Iceland. Presumably, the gods were worshipped outdoors in nature and at home in their houses, but not in specific buildings.

The saga heroes are predominantly neutral with regard to their religious persuasion; they trust in their own might and main or are noble heathens, who believe in Him, who created everything. If they encounter Christianity, they are converted. Especially in the unknown world, heathen dangers lurk: in Greenland,

46    *The Sagas of Icelanders*

in Vinland, in the Arctic Ocean–and in Götaland, Sweden. It was mentioned above (p. 16) how in *Bard's Saga,* Odin appears in disguise on a ship in the Arctic Ocean and preaches Christianity to a priest but disappears when the priest hits him on the head with his crucifix. In *Eirik the Red's Saga*, the people on the Vinland expedition fall ill after consuming the meat of a whale, because the heathen Thorhall invoked "Old Redbeard," his "guardian," whom he believes to be "of more help than [...] Christ" (Chapter 8). In *The Saga of Hord and the People of Holm*, Hord robs the mound of the dangerous Soti, but he cannot open the mound until he receives help from an unknown man, who turns out to be Odin (Chapter 15). At the opening of the mound, he gets hold of a cursed ring, which is the cause of his demise. The hero would have been better off without help from the heathen god.

The main event in the history of Iceland, as related in the sagas, is the introduction of Christianity. This is a turning point or demarcation between the old, heathen world and the new, Christian world. The sagas often refer to heathendom as "the old faith." One way or another, Christianity plays a significant role in almost every saga. The sagas of the Icelanders suggest that the transition from heathendom to Christianity proceeded relatively smoothly. In these sagas, the introduction of Christianity is depicted in a positive light, and symbols associated with Christianity are found in prophecies and foreboding dreams in heathen times. In *The Saga of Hord and the People of Holm*, a woman has a dream in which she sees a genealogical tree with a large flower. The dream is interpreted, and the large flower is construed as a symbol of the new faith, which will be better than the current one (Chapter 7). *Njal's Saga* conveys a distinct Christian tone and emphasizes the significance of forgiveness. Gunnar, who lived before the introduction of Christianity, finds it harder than other men to kill his enemies, which suggests a Christian principle of forgiveness. And Njal takes Hoskuld as his fosterson, even though Njal's sons have killed his father. After the introduction of Christianity and the burning, peace only becomes a reality, because Sidu-Hall refuses compensation for the killing of his son and challenges all the other influential men to act in the same manner. The forgiveness for which both Njal and Gunnar fought in vain before their death in the old world, finally replaces the blood vengeance at the end of the saga. When Christianity arrives, Njal converts and dies an almost hagiographic death in the burning of Bergthorshvol. But the acts of revenge in this saga are placed in a heathen context; they could have continued in perpetuity and become a threat to society. Similarly, the saga describes the introduction of Christianity as a dramatic event. It is believed that the saga writer here inserted a *þáttr*, *The Tale about Christianity* (*Kristni þáttr*), about the introduction of Christianity. The *þáttr* relates how heathens and Christians ride in two armed groups to the Althing. The country is divided between Christianity and heathendom, and both factions are prepared for conflict unless each is allowed to practice their own faith. The Christians are led by Gizur and Hjalti, who have been instructed by King Olaf Tryggvason to convert the Icelanders to Christianity. The king has also taken hostage the Icelanders who were in Norway. In this tense situation, Thorgeir *Ljósvetningagoði*

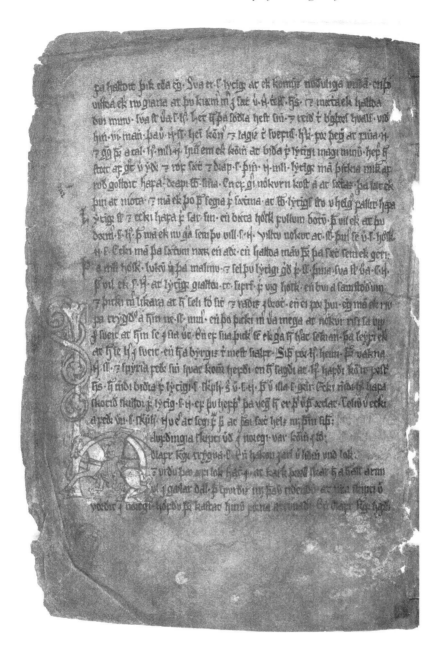

*Figure 13.1* Kálfalækjarbók, a manuscript of *Njal's Saga*, contains at the beginning of Chapter 100 one of the only illuminated capitals in a manuscript containing sagas of Icelanders. In this chapter, it is told that there has been a change of power (*hǫfðingjaskipti*) and religion in Norway. Perhaps the rider on the horse is the missionary king Olaf Tryggvason. AM 133 fol. (ca. 1350), The Árni Magnússon Institute for Icelandic Studies. Reykjavík. Photo: Jóhanna Ólafsdóttir.

48  *The Sagas of Icelanders*

("chieftain or Godi from Ljosavatn"), who holds the highest authority of the Althing and happens to be a member of the heathen faction, is to arrive at a decision; he walks away, pulls his cloak over his head, and lies down for the entire day and the following night. The next day, he announces his decision: Iceland shall have only one law, the Christian law. Tactically, this is a clever decision—but he is also under considerable pressure from the Norwegian king. The *þáttr* about the Icelandic missionary, *The Tale of Thorvald the Far-Travelled* (*Þorvalds þáttr víðfǫrla*), preserved in the saga about Olaf Tryggvason, however, portrays the Icelanders as a much more unmanageable and stubborn people, not quite ready to convert so easily. Thorvald is on an evangelizing mission with a Saxon bishop, Fridrek, who eventually gives up on both Iceland and Thorvald, since the latter kills two men after they have composed a slanderous verse about them:

> The bishop has borne
> nine children;
> Thorvald is the father
> of them all.
> (Chapter 6)

The bishop interprets the verse innocently (the reference to the bishop baptizing nine children, and Thorvald serving as their godfather), while Thorvald focuses on the defamatory meaning that suggests a sexual relationship between the two men, which leads him to kill the verse's composers. Subsequently, the bishop reminds Thorvald that Christians shall not seek revenge but endure slander and evil for the sake of God. After this event, the bishop leaves the country.

### The Family

The family relations of the saga heroes are of decisive importance for their status and abilities. The individual has an obligation to his family, just as the family has an obligation to the individual. For that reason, the many lists of ancestors and family relations in the sagas of Icelanders are not without importance. According to the law, individuals are obliged to one another in the world of the sagas.

The saga society centers on ancestry; one should preferably be able to trace one's family to an important ancestor, one of the important settlers or even further back to Sigurd Snake-Eye, Ragnar Lothbrok ("Shaggy-breeches"), or one of the other heroes in the sagas of ancient times. The sagas note whether a man or a woman comes from an important or unimportant family. In the same way, it is significant if an individual's family is not commented upon.

The world described in the sagas is a society of clans. One did not belong to two clans at the same time. Through marital relations, alliances between clans were established. A good marriage strengthens the family, whereas a bad marriage may weaken or even pose a danger to the family. When a woman is married

The Society of the Sagas of Icelanders   49

into a new family, she becomes a member of the new clan. There are, however, exceptions to the rule. When Bolli in *The Saga of the People of Laxardal* cheated his friend, fosterbrother and cousin Kjartan by marrying his truelove Gudrun, it is Bolli who moves to the bride's family—not the other way round. Here he becomes a member of Gudrun's family at Laugar. Nothing good comes from this alliance either.

**Legal Matters**

According to Ari the Learned's *Book of Icelanders*, the Icelandic Althing was established in 930. The assembly took place at Þingvellir every year in June. It was presided over by the lawspeaker (Icelandic *lǫgsǫgumaðr*), who had supreme authority regarding the contents of the laws until the laws were recorded on parchment in 1117/1118. The lawspeaker was elected for a period of three years. He had to recite the laws at the assembly, and before the laws were committed to writing, he had to know them by heart. The legislative power belonged to the *lǫgrétta* (derived from the phrase *at rétta lǫg*, literally "to right the law"), which consisted of thirty-six local chieftains with a juridical function, who each had two assessors. At a later date, the *lǫgrétta* was expanded to comprise forty-eight chieftains. The head of the *lǫgrétta* was the lawspeaker. Around 960, it was decided that Iceland should be divided into quarters. In each quarter, there were local spring-assemblies, which were held before the Althing. At the Althing, there were four quarter courts, which made up the juridical part of the assembly. Unanimity was necessary before these courts could pass judgment, which meant that many cases could not be settled. For this reason, the fifth court (Icelandic *fimmtardómr*) was established around 1000, which could arrive at majority decisions; this court functioned as a court of appeal. The legislative and judicial powers were separate. There was no executive power, and thus when a sentence had been pronounced, it was up to the plaintiff to ensure that it was carried through.

Icelandic society was divided into *goðorð* ("office of a chieftain") under the jurisdiction of a *goði* ("chieftain"; plural *goðar*). The *goði* was responsible for attending to juridical matters at the assembly, but originally the *goði* probably also fulfilled a religious function. The country was first divided into twelve juridical districts, which each consisted of three chieftaincies or *goðorð*. Accordingly, there were three chieftains in each juridical district. Until the division of the country into four quarters, there were thirty-six chieftains in Iceland. After that there were 39 since there were four juridical districts in the northern quarter but three in the other quarters. At the Althing, the chieftain had the support of his *þingmenn* ("assembly-men"). Every ninth farmer had to accompany the chieftain to the Althing, while those who remained at home were required to pay the expenses of those traveling to the assembly. A *goðorð* could either be inherited or sold. The power of a chieftain depended on his number of *þingmenn*.

50    *The Sagas of Icelanders*

The *goðorð* system was originally not geographically defined; a *þingmaðr* ("assembly-man") could belong to a chieftain living farther away, and he could terminate his association with a chieftain and obligate himself to another. This changed, however, with the division of the country into quarters; after that a chieftain could no longer have *þingmenn* from outside his quarter. A *þingmaðr* promised the chieftain his support, while in return the chieftain promised the *þingmaðr* his protection.

In the best of worlds laws are obeyed. At the end of a saga, a settlement is often reached, and peace and order are reestablished in the local society. But the sagas also describe how the legal community is corrupt. There are often economical interests at stake, when a magnate attempts to outlaw a man, because if he succeeds, he can take over his property. In *Njal's Saga*, the case against those responsible for the burning is thwarted by quibbling, which results in a bloody battle of the entire crowd at the assembly. *The Saga of the Confederates* provides a sophisticated and satirical commentary on the judges' lack of idealism and not least their corruption.

### Gender

Society in the sagas is extremely divided in respect to gender. In *The Saga of the People of Laxardal*, it is grounds for divorce, if a woman wears trousers or if a man wears a shirt with such a wide neckline that his nipples show. The saga has a word for it not found anywhere else: "divorce neckline" (*brautgangshǫfuðsmátt*). While men traveled and took part in assembly matters, the domain of women was the farm. Women took care of housekeeping and the preparation of goods derived from domestic animals, among other things the production of *vaðmál* ("homespun"), a homemade fabric of wool, which was exported to foreign countries and also served as a means of payment. During his travels abroad, the man could achieve honor and wealth and thereby strengthen his position at home in Iceland. It is not uncommon for a saga hero to get betrothed immediately before he sails away from the country. Typically, an arrangement is made that his betrothed shall wait for him for three years, after which she is free to marry someone else. Women could inherit and own land. When she was to get married, she received a dowry from her own family, which she could keep, if she got divorced, although her former husband was not always quick to pay it (as in *The Saga of the People of Vopnafjord*, Chapter 6). A woman had no say in choosing a husband, but it is a hard and fast rule in the sagas of Icelanders that nothing good comes of a marriage entered against a woman's will. Generally, a suitor (or his representatives) negotiates with the girl's father, after which the girl is asked. A suitor can also negotiate with the girl's brothers, and if the father has died, it is not uncommon for a mother to consult with her sons, as is the case in *Valla-Ljot's Saga* (Chapter 1). Some women are so proud that their fathers find it advisable to let them decide for themselves. This is the case in *The Saga of the People of Laxardal*, when Olaf Peacock proposes to Egil Skallagrimsson's daughter Thorgerd. Egil answers that Olaf has both a good family (the Irish king is his maternal grandfather) and attractive looks: "But the question will have to be taken up with Thorgerd, because there's no man who could make Thorgerd his wife should she be set against it" (Chapter 23). When Hallgerd is betrothed to Gunnar in *Njal's Saga*, her father, too, has learned that it is wisest to ask for her opinion before he arranges a marriage. She was not asked before her first marriage, and it ended in disaster. Nonetheless, introductory negotiations also take place a second time between men, where her father and paternal uncle mention her good and bad qualities before Hallgerd is summoned (Chapter 13). On the way back from her first wedding, Hallgerd laughs; both here and elsewhere in the sagas of Icelanders, laughter is not a sign of joy. Rather, it is an expression of anger and frustration.

The sagas of Icelanders are primarily interested in the strong and courageous men of the past. They dwell on the male hero's appearance, whereas they tend to have little to say about the appearance of women. One of the most magnificent heroes in the sagas, Gunnar in *Njal's Saga*, is presented as follows:

> Gunnar Hamundarson lived at Hlidarendi in Fljotshlid. He was big and strong and an excellent fighter. He could swing a sword and throw a spear with either hand, if he wished, and he was so swift with a sword that there seemed to be three in the air at once. He could shoot with a bow better than anyone else, and he always hit what he aimed at. He could jump higher than his own height, in full fighting gear, and just as far backward as forward. He swam like a seal, and there was no sport in which there was any point in competing with him. It was said that no man was his match. He was handsome and fair of skin and had a straight nose, turned up at its tip. He was blue-eyed and keen-eyed and ruddy-cheeked. His hair was thick, blond, and well-combed. He was very courteous, firm in all ways, generous and even-tempered, a true friend but a discriminating friend. He was very well off for property.
>
> (Chapter 19)

This detailed description of Gunnar is among the longest presentations of a hero in the sagas of Icelanders. It shows very well the kind of attributes considered important for the male hero of saga society: physical strength, excellent fighting skills, a handsome appearance, wealth, a pleasant temperament, and virtuous conduct. In addition, a man should preferably be popular and from a good family.

Although the sagas of Icelanders are interested primarily in the world of men, they are also populated by magnificent and proud women. The sagas are written from a male perspective, and the main female protagonists are generally given less attention, which is reflected in the description of these women. Even the depiction of Gudrun Osvifsdottir, the protagonist in *The Saga of the People of*

52  *The Sagas of Icelanders*

*Laxardal*, is short. No information is provided about her eyes, nose, hair color, or skin. The description of her is approximately half as long as that of Gunnar:

> Gudrun [...] was the most beautiful woman ever to have grown up in Iceland, and no less clever than she was good-looking. She took great care with her appearance, so much so that the adornments of other women were considered to be mere child's play in comparison. She was the shrewdest of women, highly articulate, and generous as well.
>
> (Chapter 32)

When one compares the two depictions, it is among other things noticeable that it is not said about Gunnar that he is "shrewd" or "articulate," which is emphasized in the description of Gudrun. Gunnar is characterized as a sympathetic and physically strong fellow without much intellectual capacity, which the saga also confirms. The sagas' characterizations of individuals can always be trusted; they are never contradicted by the plot of the saga. Accordingly, a theme is sometimes suggested by the description of individuals or the outcome of the action itself. If one reads about a hero that despite his good qualities, he was not a lucky man, then we know it is a sign that he will not fare well. One of the most famous characterizations is found in *Njal's Saga*, where Hrut comments on the appearance of Hallgerd, his half-brother's daughter. He does not understand, he says, how her thief's eyes have come into the family (Chapter 1). Hallgerd is only a little girl playing on the floor, but the characterization turns out to be true: Later in the saga, she is found guilty of theft, which eventually leads to the death of Gunnar. From the description of Gudrun, however, one learns that she is shrewd and maybe too shrewd for her own good.

**Women**

Despite the highly gender segregated society in the sagas, there are many examples of what one might call flexible genders, where men and women transcend societal gender role. *The Saga of the People of Laxardal* is the only saga with a woman as its protagonist: Gudrun Osvifsdottir. In fact, this saga contains many interesting women who, to a larger or lesser degree, rebel against the limited role allotted to them by society. The saga begins with the settling of the famous settler Unn the Deep-minded. She is a widow and establishes a farm at Breidafjord that is worthy of a magnate. When at an advanced age she passes away, she dies sitting straight and upright on her high-seat (Chapter 7). The protagonist of the saga, Gudrun, stays within the frame of female roles, since she never takes up arms—she has men doing that for her. But that her power is at least as great as that of men can be seen in the wedding scene, when she marries for the fourth time. A conflict arises when her husband Thorkel wants to kill Gunnar, the Slayer of Thidrandi (*Þiðrandabani*), an outlaw, whom Gudrun has promised

The Society of the Sagas of Icelanders    53

to protect. Without hesitation, she gets up from the table in her bridal gown to stop Thorkel, and she is successful. But when it is necessary to take up arms, she sends off her brothers, her husband, or her sons. Another woman in the saga who challenges her female role is Kjartan's sister Thurid. She is unhappily married to a Norwegian, and the couple have a little daughter. But he deserts Thurid and intends to sail back to Norway. When Thurid's peace-loving father has left his farm, she rides off to take matters into her own hands. The men are asleep, when she arrives, she slips on board the ship, takes her husband's sword, puts their daughter in its place, and sneaks away. The girl's crying wakes him up, and he demands his sword back. When Thurid refuses to give it to him, he puts a curse on it. The sword, which Thurid gives to her cousin Bolli after his return to Iceland, is later used to kill Kjartan. Both the Norwegian and the young daughter are lost in a shipwreck at sea before their arrival in Norway (Chapter 30). In the same saga, one also meets the woman Aud, who "was neither good-looking nor exceptional in other ways" (Chapter 32), as the saga says. She is most nastily tricked by Gudrun and her own husband Thord, who has little affection for her, and who married her because of her great wealth. Gudrun starts a false rumor that Aud "wears breeches with a codpiece and long leggings" (Chapter 35), and Thord uses this as a reason for divorcing Aud to marry Gudrun. To wear trousers as a woman, as mentioned above, is grounds for divorce. To avenge herself, Aud actually does put on trousers, rides off, and wounds Thord's arm and both of his nipples with a short sword. This is hardly a coincidence: She, who is accused of being masculine, wounds him exactly in a place that emasculates him symbolically. Evidently, the saga writer is impressed with this woman, for when she rides off, he comments that now she was "dressed in breeches, to be sure" (Chapter 35). Unn the Deep-minded, Gudrun, Thurid, and Aud, however, are not the only strong women either in *The Saga of the People of Laxardal* or in the sagas of Icelanders in general.

Hallgerd in *Njal's Saga* may also be said to be a rebel. When her father arranges a marriage against her will, she makes her foster father kill the man (Chapter 11). While Njal and Gunnar love peace, their wives initiate quarrels and orchestrate killings in each other's households, escalating into a bloody conflict that spirals out of control. Hallgerd cannot forgive Gunnar for having slapped her in the face because she has stolen. As a result, she causes his death in his last battle. His bowstring breaks, and when he asks her to twist a new one using her long hair, she flatly refuses and refers to the slap in the face (Chapters 48 and 77). In contrast to the women in *The Saga of the People of Laxardal*, Hallgerd does not have the respect or sympathy of the saga writer.

The women mentioned here belong to the upper stratum of society; they are daughters of magnates and/or are married to magnates. But one also meets another type of woman in the sagas: those on the periphery of society who use magic to impose their will. They are often unmarried or widows, but sometimes they are simply individuals of humble means. In *The Saga of the Sworn*

54   *The Sagas of Icelanders*

*Brothers*, Thorgrim makes passes at the daughter of Grima, who is considered skilled in witchcraft. She asks him to discontinue the improper relationship, but he keeps showing up, so she sets her slave on him—though not until she has made the slave immune to weapons by "pass[ing] her hands […] over his body" (Chapter 15). Later in the same saga, the reader meets yet another woman of the same type, also called Grima, this time in Greenland; she is also skilled in various crafts. She has a chair with a carved image of Thor, and when Thormod sits down on it, he becomes invisible (Chapter 40). In *The Saga of the Slayings on the Heath*, Bardi's fostermother, "a wise woman," uses the same kind of magic as the first Grima in *The Saga of the Sworn Brothers*. Before a great battle, she touches Bardi all over, "on the top of his head" and "all the way down to his toes," before she gives him a necklace and the instruction not to alter anything (Chapter 23). In *Kormak's saga*, Thordis on Spakonufjall (literally "Prophetess' mountain") is able to blunt swords, so that they cannot "cut at all" (Chapter 23). In *The Saga of the People of Vatnsdal*, the region is bullied by Ljot, who "had little enough in common with ordinary good-natured folk" and her son (Chapter 18). To save her son, she uses magic:

> She had pulled her clothes up over her head and was walking backwards with her head thrust between her legs. The look in her eyes was hideous—the way she could dart them like a troll.
>
> (Chapter 26)

These sorceresses are dishonorable women, as indicated by their names in some sagas. Magic is the power of the powerless. In *Gold-Thorir's Saga*, the two witches are called Thurid *Drikkin* ("dungcheek") and Kerling ("hag"). Kerling knows the same tricks as Ljot in the abovementioned example. When Thurid Drikkin attempts to stop her, the two engage in an unheroic fight:

> Then Thurid Drikkin saw Kerling walking around behind the house with her clothes pulled up and her head bent down, looking backwards through her legs at the clouds. Thurid then leapt out of the fortification, attacked her, and grabbed her hair, tearing the flesh off the back of her neck. Kerling grabbed Thurid's ear with both hands and tore off the ear and the flesh of her cheek below it. And at that moment Thorir's weapons began to bite, and they did a lot of harm.
>
> (Chapter 17)

Only later is Kerling slain: Gold-Thorir throws a large slab of rock after her, which hits her between the legs and causes her death. It is hard to imagine a more humiliating demise.

In the sagas of Icelanders, honorable women rarely resort to fighting or taking up arms. Instead, they send off their men to take vengeance. Aud, who independently avenges her humiliating divorce, is an exception. In *Gisli Sursson's Saga*,

*The Society of the Sagas of Icelanders*    55

Gisli's sister Thordis also attempts to get at her brother's killer, but she manages to inflict only a wound on his leg. In the same saga, Gisli's wife Aud tries to fight by his side in his last battle, but her fighting abilities are insufficient, which is reflected in his last words to her:

> I knew long ago that I had married well, but never realised till now that the match was as good as this. Yet the help you gave me now was less than you wished and less than you intended, even though the blow was good, for I might have dispatched both men in the same way.
>
> (Chapter 34)

Gisli loves and respects his wife for good reasons, but despite her exceptional efforts, he nonetheless points out that they were insufficient.

Still, the women are as keen as the men on preserving their own and the family's honor, even though they do not physically fight to preserve it. If their men or brothers do not preserve the family's honor, the woman has certain ways to force them to do so. In *Njal's Saga*, the sons of Njal have killed Hildigunn's husband and Njal's foster son Hoskuld. Earlier in the saga, Hildigunn is portrayed as "an unusually tough and harsh-tempered woman, but a fine woman when she had to be" (Chapter 95). She is the niece of Flosi, whom she has invited, because she wants to force him to avenge Hoskuld:

> Hildigunn then went to the hall and opened up her chest and took from it the cloak which Flosi had given Hoskuld, and in which Hoskuld was slain, and which she had kept there with all its blood. She then went back into the main room with the cloak. She walked silently up to Flosi. Flosi had finished eating and the table had been cleared. Hildigunn placed the cloak on Flosi's shoulders; the dried blood poured down all over him. Then she spoke: "This cloak, Flosi, was your gift to Hoskuld, and now I give it back to you. He was slain in it. In the name of God and all good men I charge you, by all the wonders of your Christ and by your courage and manliness, to avenge all the wounds which he received in dying – or else suffer the contempt of all men." Flosi flung off the cloak and threw it into her arms and said, "You are a monster and want us to take the course which will be worst for us all – cold are the counsels of women." Flosi was so stirred that his face was in turns as red as blood, as pale as grass, and as black as Hel itself.
>
> (Chapter 116)

Flosi does not want to carry out the revenge, but since Hildigunn has challenged his honor, he no longer has a choice. The result is the burning, in which Njal and his entire household perish, except for Kari. The final reconciliation between the conflicting parties takes place at the end of the saga when Kari and Hildigunn marry.

56    *The Sagas of Icelanders*

The vindictive woman, who with her provocations incites her male relative to take vengeance is a type of woman found in several sagas. Scholars have dubbed this kind of woman *die Hetzerin* or "the whetter." Gudrun Osvifsdottir uses this method in order to coerce her husband and brothers to kill Kjartan:

> Gudrun replied, "With your temperament, you'd have made some farmer a good group of daughters, fit to do no one any good or any harm. After all the abuse and shame Kjartan has heaped upon you, you don't let it disturb your sleep while he goes riding by under your very noses, with only one other man to accompany him. Such men have no better memory than a pig. There's not much chance you'll ever dare to make a move against Kjartan at home if you won't even stand up to him now, when he only has one or two others to back him up. The lot of you just sit here at home, making much of yourselves, and one could only wish there were fewer of you."
>
> (Chapter 48)

Gudrun's provocative words are a traditionally symbolic criticism of their manhood, as a man's honor is intimately connected to his masculinity.

### Unmanly Men and the Limitation of Men's Roles

It is extremely rare to find a man in a woman's role. In the sagas of Icelanders, the status of women is generally lower than that of men, if they are of the same class. It was truly risky for men to step out of the male role, because they could then be exposed to *nið* ("scorn"), which might result in the loss of honor. In the quotation above, Hildigunn accused Flosi of being an object of contempt to everyone (a *níðingr*); such a man has no honor. *Nið* is a stereotypical and symbolic accusation of unmanliness; when directed against a man, it marks him as a contemptuous person, but when directed against a woman, it signals that she is promiscuous. The most serious attacks on a man's honor were of a sexual nature. The purpose of *nið* was to expose a man as being unmanly through references to his effeminacy. This effeminacy could be realized as homosexuality (the most humiliating was the passive or "female" part in a sexual male relationship) or femininity/softness or comparisons with animals giving birth. A classical example of *nið* is found in *Gisli Sursson's Saga*, where Skeggi, one of the suitors of Gisli's sister Thordis wants to have an effigy in the likeness of Gisli and Kolbjorn made, "and one shall stand behind the other, and this *nið* shall remain forever to scorn them" (Chapter 2). Despite the scorn, Skeggi is lucky and manages to keep his life; he only loses one leg, which is chopped off. Accusations of this kind were so serious that they demanded revenge, and in some cases, according to the laws, even blood vengeance, if three particularly crude words were used: *ragr*, *stroðinn*, and *sorðinn*. *Ragr* designates a willingness to play the "female" part in a sexual relationship, while both *stroðinn* and *sorðinn* (past participles of *streða* and *serða*, respectively) designate a man, who has been used sexually by another man.

*The Society of the Sagas of Icelanders*   57

The purpose of the *nið*-accusations was to label symbolically a man as a contemptuous person. Even though sexual symbolism was used in the accusations, the kernel of *nið* was not sexual. The sexual part only serves as a powerful symbol in order to illustrate the unmanly man—in point of fact, the unnatural and immoral conduct, which underlies the crimes that are so serious that they are called *níðingsverk* ("villain's work"). The "unmanliness" with regard to sexuality symbolizes the incomplete fulfillment of the male role.

The *nið* does not always have sexual overtones. It is sufficient to suggest that a man behaves like a little girl, a weak old woman, or a farmer's daughter, as Gudrun tells her brothers to great effect. When Gunnar in *Njal's Saga* is accused of having cried, when a man rode into him, instead of taking revenge, it is also an accusation of unmanliness (Chapter 53). As soon as the accusation has been voiced, Gunnar is obliged to take revenge. In *The Saga of Hrafnkel Frey's Godi*, a female servant mocks Hrafnkel, for not having taken revenge: "It is true what old folks say that the older you get, the feebler you become" (Chapter 14). According to the woman, men lose their manliness with age, because they become more cowardly. Her words cause Hrafnkel to kill Sam's innocent brother Eyvind, who is not involved in the conflict, against his will. In the same way, the old and blind Egil Skallagrimsson becomes the object of the female servants' mockery, when he stumbles around by the fire on his stiff legs (Chapter 88). And when the hero in *The Saga of the People of Floi* as an old man comes riding—huddled over because of a cold headwind—a pompous Norwegian laughs at him, because "it hardly shows […] that [he was] once called a champion" (Chapter 34).

Nonetheless, the sagas of Icelanders provide examples of men, who challenge the male role. Njal is a famous example. Even after mocking verses about his beardlessness have been composed, which are an accusation of femininity, he refuses to seek vengeance. The most pronounced example, however, is found in *The Saga of the People of Floi*. The hero Thorgils has gone to Greenland with his family, where they are unable to find the settled areas and therefore die of hunger and illness. One day, when Thorgils returns after exploring the inland ice together with two others, he finds his wife stabbed to death at home in their hut. This happens shortly after she has given birth to a little boy. The men hear a gurgling sound in the darkness; this is the newborn trying to nurse at his mother's breast. Thorgils then cuts open his nipples and starts milking. First blood comes out, but after a while a whitish liquid appears. On this he feeds his little son. The boy is raised with the three surviving men and becomes a stoic little guy; however, he ends his life sadly when they finally manage to leave Greenland and sail back to Iceland. The father is overcome by grief and refuses to part with the corpse, so that the boy can be buried, which, of course, is unchristian. His travel companions lure him away and bury the boy in a church yard. Thorgils then utters the unforgettable words that from now on he will never blame women for loving their breast-fed children more than others.

58   *The Sagas of Icelanders*

## Love

One of the basic themes in the sagas of Icelanders is love, a topic that the saga writers continuously circle around—aside from life's other challenges, such as honor, violence, justice, greed, and forgiveness. In 1971, Thomas Bredsdorff published the book *Chaos and Love: The Philosophy of the Icelandic Family Sagas* (the English translation was published in 2001), in which he demonstrated how in many sagas the power of love unleashes chaos and thereby threatens the sagas' social order, when the love is unrestrained or goes against societal rules. A subgroup of the sagas of Icelanders, the skalds' sagas, focus from beginning to end on the skalds' conflicted and unhappy love life. The group consists first and foremost of *The Saga of Gunnlaug Serpent-Tongue, The Saga of Hallfred the Troublesome Poet, Kormak's saga*, and *The Saga of Bjorn, Champion of the Hitardal People*. Early on in these sagas, the skalds fall madly in love with a woman, whom they never marry for a variety of reasons. But they cannot get the woman out of their minds and compose stanzas about unfulfilled love. In *Kormak's saga*, a curse is placed on Kormak, so that he will never marry Steingerd, the woman he loves. In *The Saga of Gunnlaug Serpent-Tongue*, Gunnlaug's leg is dislocated, so that he cannot show up at the wedding and thereby prevent the marriage of his truelove Helga and his rival. In *The Saga of Hallfred the Troublesome Poet*, Hallfred does not want to marry Kolfinna when he gets the offer, but still he cannot stop thinking about her. And in *The Saga of Bjorn, Champion of the Hitardal People*, Bjorn is betrayed by his rival, who untruthfully claims that he is dead, so that he can marry Oddny. The women love the skalds, and despite their marriage to other men, they always remain in the skalds' thoughts. The skalds visit them, flirt with them, seduce them, and sometimes impregnate them, even though they are married. Although the skalds challenge the societal order in some ways by prioritizing their own feelings, they nonetheless have the saga writer's sympathy. Usually, the skalds have good reasons to persevere, for due to arbitrary circumstances they cannot marry their beloved. These are sagas about unhappy love. Usually, however, the marriage settlement is a serious, social contract between two families. As a general rule, it is not an arrangement made on the basis of an impetuous love affair similar to that of the skalds, even though it is clear that love must exist—or develop—between the spouses. Gunnar and Hallgerd marry after they have fallen in love at the Althing, but the marriage brings endless problems with it. It is a "a lustful marriage" (*girndarráð*), and not an example to be followed. The narrators often comment, however, that spouses come to love each other after the wedding, as in *The Saga of the People of Reykjadal and of Killer-Skuta* (Chapter 11) and *The Saga of the People of Laxardal* (Chapter 7). Similarly, it is worthy of comment, if there is no love, but rather coolness between the spouses. When Thorgils in *The Saga of the People of Floi* marries late in life, his young wife is not pleased. There is coolness between them, and she moves home to her

The Society of the Sagas of Icelanders    59

father for a while. Their relationship does not improve until the spouses watch a fight between a hen and a rooster and Thorgils comments that it reminds him of them (Chapters 30 and 31). The ideal is for marriage and love to be united.

Gisli and Aud's marriage is an example of an ideal marriage. The two treat each other more or less as equals. When there is talk in the women's room about Aud having once had an affair with Gisli's brother-in-law Thorgrim, Aud subsequently speaks openly with Gisli about it—in contrast to her sister-in-law Asgerd. Asgerd is married to Gisli's brother Thorkel but has a secret affair with Vestein. In contrast to Aud, she lies to her husband about the matter, but since he has overheard the women's conversation and is angry in the evening, she threatens to divorce him (Chapter 9). The revelation of Asgerd's love affair impairs Thorkel's honor, and his solution is to kill Vestein. Nonetheless, it is not known whether it was Thorkel or Thorgrim, Gisli's brother-in-law, who did the killing— this is the crime's riddle in the saga. Vestein is Gisli's friend, and in revenge Gisli kills Thorgrim, for naturally he cannot take revenge against his own brother. Or is it perhaps that Gisli takes revenge against Thorgrim because he once had an affair with his wife? Aud remains a loyal wife throughout the saga. When Gisli has been outlawed, she hides him, and when one of Gisli's enemies tries to bribe her into revealing Gisli's whereabouts, Aud rams the money purse offered to her against his nose, so that blood spurts out. Gisli's sister Thordis does not have the same harmonious love relationship as her brother and his wife. In fact, Gisli seems to consider it necessary to commit several killings to restore the honor of the family, viewing it as a means of rectifying the fallout from Thordis's affairs, which appear to be motivated more by infatuation than concern for the family. Gisli attacks a total of four men with whom she has had a relationship. First, he kills Bard, who is said to have seduced Thordis. Then he maims Skeggi, who courted Thordis. After that, he kills Kolbjorn, who had relations with her. And finally, he kills Thordis's husband, Thorgrim, while he is lying in bed with her. It is perhaps understandable that she reveals Gisli as the killer to her new husband, Bork, even though she regrets it after Gisli's death.

For love relationships to function in the sagas, the two spouses should preferably be of equal social standing. Nothing good comes of marriages, in which the man has much money but the woman more honor—that is, nothing good for the man. Money or wealth cannot compensate for the man's lack of honor or the woman's lack of love, even though attempts are made to do so. When Gudrun Osvifsdottir gets married for the first time to a man, who is a nonentity compared to her, it is a condition that he gives her everything she wants.

> Thorvald […] was a wealthy man but hardly a hero. He asked for Gudrun Osvifsdottir's hand […] His suit was not rejected but Osvif felt the difference in their means would be evident in the marriage conditions. […] Gudrun was eventually betrothed to Thorvald according to conditions which Osvif himself decided upon. He declared that Gudrun should control their common

60　*The Sagas of Icelanders*

finances once they were married and would acquire the right to half of the estate, whether the marriage was a brief or lengthy one. Thorvald was also obliged to purchase whatever finery Gudrun required in order that no other woman of equal wealth should own better, although not to the point of ruining the farm. [...] Gudrun was not asked for her opinion and, although she was rather against the idea, nothing was done. [...] Gudrun cared little for Thorvald and was avid in demanding purchases of precious objects. There were no treasures in all the West Fjords so costly that Gudrun felt she did not deserve them, and vented her anger on Thorvald if he failed to buy them, however dear they were.

(Chapter 34)

Despite the costly purchases, Thorvald has no chance of earning either Gudrun's love or respect. As expected, her marriage to Thorvald ends in divorce.

In the same saga, Gudrun and Kjartan love each other very much. Because of a disagreement between them, the proud Gudrun does not promise to wait for him while he travels to Norway. Nonetheless, she waits. And it is only with the help of force and cheating that Bolli, Kjartan's friend, foster brother, and cousin, manages to marry her. The father puts pressure on Gudrun, and Bolli makes her believe that Kjartan may never return to Iceland because of his very intimate relationship with the king's sister; he even insinuates that Kjartan and the king's sister may marry. Even though Kjartan and the king's sister may well be in love, Kjartan returns home, for he has not forgotten Gudrun, but there he finds Gudrun married to his best friend. The thwarted love, the betrayal, and the jealousy lead to a series of humiliations on the part of both families, which reach their climax when Gudrun sends off her brothers and Bolli to kill Kjartan. When Gudrun's son, Bolli, at the end of the saga asks Gudrun, who by then is an old woman and has lived through four marriages, whom of her men she loved the most, she answers: "I was worst to the one I loved the most" (Chapter 78). As a reader, one suspects that she is thinking of Kjartan. This is a heartbreaking account of how love and honor can collide—with a tragic ending.

**Economy and Honor**

An individual's honor and the plot of a saga are often closely associated with the relationship of an individual to money and wealth. Money is not to be understood in today's meaning: the sagas' economic capital—in addition to land, buildings, and ships—is comprised of gold, silver, cattle, and homespun wool, which in the world of the sagas was a general means of payment and an important export commodity. In the sagas, gold and silver are measured according to weight, marks, and ounces, both of which are a unit of weight (one mark is ca. 204–215 grams, one ounce ca. 26–27 grams). The ideal saga hero is wealthy, but even though wealth and respect are often connected in the

*The Society of the Sagas of Icelanders*  61

world of the sagas, this is not always the case and can lead to problems. If a saga hero does not have the opportunity to achieve both wealth and respect, but has to choose, he must choose honor, which is what Killer-Glum advises Ogmund Bash to do in *The Tale of Ogmund Bash* (*Ögmundar þáttr dytts ok Gunnars helmings*), when the latter sails off to Norway. But Ogmund does not heed his advice and acquires a lot of wealth on his journey, while at the same time he jeopardizes his honor. When he returns to Iceland, he behaves as if his honor were intact, until Killer-Glum makes it clear to him that he no longer wants to see him, unless he has restored his honor. In other words, it is necessary to guard one's honor and not believe that the improvement of one's economy replaces the loss of honor.

In the value system of the sagas, it is possible to be honorless and wealthy at the same time. If a man is a freed slave or a descendant of a freed slave, it is generally not possible for him to achieve the same social status as a man from a good family. Sometimes, it is even possible to discern astonishment by saga writers, when they present wealthy people descended from slaves: "Thorgeir was the name of a man. He lived at Thorgeirsfell. He was very rich in livestock but in reality a freed slave" (*Eirik the Red's Saga*, Chapter 3; my translation).

In *Hen-Thorir's Saga*, the imbalance between honor and wealth ends in catastrophe. Hen-Thorir is not from a good family and has few friends, but he manages to make himself economically secure. Hen-Thorir is an upstart. Generally, the most important individuals in a saga are presented with information about family relations, but about Hen-Thorir it is only told:

> There was a man named Thorir, who once was poor and not very well liked by most people. In the summers he had gone on trading trips between districts, selling in one what he had bought in another. In a short time he had accumulated a great deal of wealth from his dealings. [...] he became so wealthy that he had large sums of money lent out to almost everyone. Even though he had accumulated a great deal of money, his lack of popularity continued, so that there was scarcely a man more detested than was Hen-Thorir.
>
> (Chapter 1)

Hen-Thorir does not earn money through his own work; he is a loan shark. Hen-Thorir is incapable of honoring the ethical demands that accompany great wealth, whereas Blund-Ketil, an honorable and respected chieftain, is able to do so. During a famine, when the farmers in the district need supplies, Blund-Ketil kills his own animals to be able to sell some of his hay to his tenant farmers, but new tenant farmers keep arriving, and Blund-Ketil cannot continue in this way. Accordingly, he pays a visit to Hen-Thorir, who has lots of supplies, in order to make him sell to the tenant farmers. Blund-Ketil makes Hen-Thorir an offer that is both honorable and generous, but Hen-Thorir is selfish and stingy and refuses to sell to people in need. In the end, they simply

## 62    *The Sagas of Icelanders*

take the hay—after they have figured out what Thorir can do without—but being the honorable men that they are and not thieves, they provide money for the value of the hay. Nonetheless, Thorir attempts to have Blund-Ketil summoned for theft, but is unable to involve any chieftains in the case until Thorvald does so on the condition that he will receive half of Hen-Thorir's wealth. The conflict ends in a catastrophe: Hen-Thorir burns Blund-Ketil in his home. The saga shows how Hen-Thorir's miserliness and selfishness invalidates the social order and sends enormous waves through the local society, including both murder and burning. The saga shows not only what can happen, when wretched people achieve wealth, but also how wealth can lead good people to commit criminal acts.

In the world of the sagas, generosity is an ideal. *The Tale of Audun from the West Fjords* (*Auðunar þáttr vestfirzka*), which deals with the poor Audun and the Danish King Svend Estridsen, is a study in gift-giving and generosity. Audun uses all his money to buy a polar bear for the Danish king without demanding anything in return, and the king reveals his royal magnanimity by rewarding him for the bear with even greater generosity: He gives him a ship, but in case the ship should be wrecked, he gives him also a purse full of silver, and in case Audun should lose the purse in a shipwreck, he finally gives him an arm ring of gold. When Audun visits the Norwegian King Harald Hardradi (*harðráði*), the king admits that he would not have matched Svend's generosity. The portrayal of Bolli, son of Gudrun and Bolli, in *The Saga of the People of Laxardal*, clearly shows how generosity cements a man's position and popularity:

> It was soon apparent that Bolli was a man of ambition, who intended to be a leader among men. This he managed to do, not the least through his generosity. He was soon held in high esteem in Norway. That winter in Nidaros Bolli kept a company of men, and was recognised at once whenever he went drinking, as his men were better armed and dressed than the other townspeople. He alone paid for the drinks of all his company when they went drinking. This was typical of his generosity and grand style.
>
> (Chapter 73)

In contrast, stinginess is disgraceful—even downright ridiculous, as demonstrated in *The Saga of Havard of Isafjord*, where the wealthy miser Atli hides in the freezing cold in a haystack, while his wife gives everything in the storehouse to Havard (Chapter 15). However, some time with his wife under the warm bed covers makes him as generous a person as the day is long. The most famous miser in saga literature is Egil Skallagrimsson, who is not a dishonorable person. By contrast, his poet friend Einar *Skálaglamm* ("bowl-rattle") is generous and serves as a model with regard to money: "He was generous but usually had scant means, and was a firm character and a noble man" (*Egil's Saga*, Chapter 81). It does not hurt Einar's honor, that most often he has no money—because money

*The Society of the Sagas of Icelanders* 63

becomes scarce because of his generosity. But Egil is different. Because of his avarice, he keeps his father's part of the settlement, which King Athelstan pays for his dead brother (Chapter 59). And when Skallagrim asks for his part, Egil mockingly answers:

> Are you very short of money, father? I wasn't aware. I shall let you have silver as soon as I know that you need it, but I know you have kept a chest or two aside, full of silver.
>
> (Chapter 59)

In response, Skallagrim hides his valuables—a chest and a pot full of silver—immediately before his death, so that Egil cannot inherit them. Old Skallagrim is placed in a burial mound, but Egil is too stingy to provide him with valuable grave goods: "It is not mentioned whether any money was put into his tomb" (Chapter 59). Egil Skallagrimsson's attitude toward money almost crosses the line in its cynicism. As an octogenarian, who walks with difficulty, is hard of hearing and blind, Egil plans a last, remarkable feat: He wants to bring the two chests full of King Athelstan's silver to the Althing, where he intends to scatter the silver at the Law Rock, when the crowd is at its largest:

> "I'll be very much surprised," [Egil mumbles], "if they all share it out fairly amongst themselves. I expect there'll be plenty of pushing and shoving. It might even end with the whole Thing breaking out in a brawl."
>
> (Chapter 88)

With this last act, Egil wants to reveal the fundamental greed of all the magnates, which will be destructive of their honor and lead to discord and chaos. But his mad plan—in the words of his son-in-law—is thwarted. In the end, the saga writer lets Egil bury his silver before he dies, just like his father before him. The saga ends by confirming the Christian moral precept that money should be treated with disdain and indifference, and that the magnates' supposed, but untested greed, must be controlled for the benefit of society.

### The Farm

In the sagas, the farm constitutes the frame around daily life. The household consists of the farmer, his wife, their children, and grandparents, but also workers, servants, and slaves. Workers could rent land from the farmers; they were the so-called tenant farmers, who were not well off. Many bloody conflicts stem from farm work, when, for example, a neighbor lets his animals graze on the other side of the field boundary or if animals disappeared. It is not uncommon for saga heroes to show a certain disdain for farm life, when they return from their lives as members of the Norwegian king's retinue. In *The Saga of Bjorn,*

64   *The Sagas of Icelanders*

*Champion of the Hitardal People*, Bjorn picks up a newborn calf—and it is not long before his rival and enemy Thord uses it against him:

> They went off and came to the byres, and Thorgeir stepped in first because he knew the way better. But a cow had borne a calf, and Thorgeir tripped over the calf as it lay on the floor, and cursed. Bjorn told him to throw the calf up into the stall, but Thorgeir said that the lower the devil lay the better, and would not touch it. Then Bjorn picked up the calf from the floor and threw it into the stall. Home they went then, and Thorgeir told his friends how Bjorn had picked up the calf from the floor and thrown it up into the stall, "but I wouldn't touch it." There were guests there who heard Thorgeir's story. And not much later these same people visited Thord at Hitarnes and told him this. He spoke, saying that Bjorn had got enough people, both men and women, to see to such things so that there should be no need for him to act as midwife to the cows, and he spoke a verse:

> Why must you, O mighty
> mud-dweller, keep casting
> (though a seal has scratched me)
> scorn on my wounding?
> You'll be sorry, soldier
> at sight of shield shaking,
> you clutched a twisted calf beneath
> a cow's tail, dung-encrusted.

> People thought it wise that this verse should not be spread about, but it was not kept secret, and it came to Bjorn's ears. He thought it a malicious verse, and he was not willing to let it rest.
>
> (Chapter 16)

Earlier in the same saga, Bjorn's rival Thord wants to catch a seal in a hole in the ice—presumably an easy catch—but the seal bites him, and the wound swells and becomes infected. Bjorn, of course, composes a mocking verse about this incident. It is almost a theme in *The Saga of Bjorn, Champion of the Hitardal People* how the former heroes of the king's retinue do not thrive as farmers in Iceland.

In *Valla-Ljot's Saga*, a disagreement arises about who should walk out into the mud to fetch a sow. The chieftain considers it beneath him and believes that it is the duty of a freed slave, who, incidentally, is to marry his mother. When the freed slave compares his courage with that of the sow, the chieftain is forced to fetch it—but he subsequently kills the freed slave (Chapter 1).

The dwelling during the Age of Settlement was the *skáli* (hall): a long living room with an oblong fireplace in the middle and raised platforms along the walls,

*The Society of the Sagas of Icelanders* 65

where one sat during the day and slept at night. Often, the sleeping area could be closed off. After the Age of Settlement, the *skáli* was expanded to include more rooms. The most important source of information about dwellings in the Age of Settlement is archaeological excavations, not the sagas. In the museum Reykjavík 871 ± 2 in the center of Reykjavík, one can today see an excavated farm, a *skáli*, which has been dated to the earliest years of settlement. The farm Stöng, abandoned after volcanic ashes rained down from Hekla in 1104, is another example, which can be seen in Þjórsárdalur in the southern part of Iceland.

These excavations show that the farms changed from the beginning of the Age of Settlement through the Saga Age, and until the sagas of Icelanders were written in the thirteenth century. The description of the farms in the sagas reflects the type of farm the saga writers knew in their own times—like the farm Stöng. In other words, the descriptions of the farms in the sagas are anachronistic.

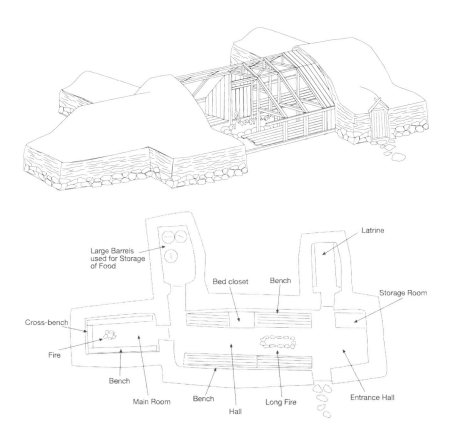

*Figure 13.2* The farm Stöng. Saga Forlag, Reykjavík.

66  *The Sagas of Icelanders*

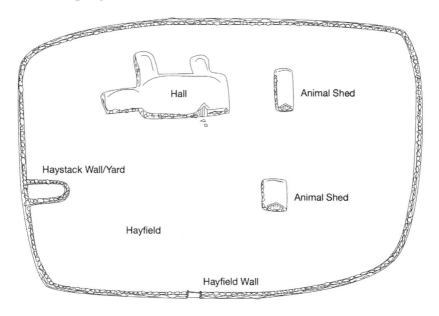

*Figure 13.3* A typical farm meadow. Saga Forlag, Reykjavík.

In Eiríksstaður in Hvammsfjörður in western Iceland, where, according to his saga, Eirik the Red lived, one can in fact see a reconstruction of a farm from the Age of Settlement. Here, there is only the main room and no adjacent rooms.

A typical farm, as described in the sagas, is surrounded by a fence, a so-called "Hayfield wall" or a "meadow fence," enclosing the farm's meadow—that is, the manured field with the best hay. The buildings of the farm are usually within the meadow-fence, but sometimes the barns are outside of the fence.

The haybarn, the enclosure where the hay is kept, is usually close to the meadow-fence. The smithy is separate from the other buildings because of fire hazard, which may also be the case with the *eldhús* (literally "fire-house"), which was a type of kitchen, but which was not used exclusively for cooking. There were fireplaces in the common living rooms, and many of the daily house chores took place there. Sometimes in the sagas, the word *eldhús* apparently refers not to a specific building but to the main building itself.

A bumpy and almost impassable dirt road now leads to the excavation of the farm Stöng. South of the farm, the farm has been reconstructed on the basis of archaeological investigations. Here one can see a farm as it looked around 1100. It is not from the time, when the sagas took place (tenth century), but it illustrates how the saga writers most likely imagined the layout of a farm. The farm Stöng has more rooms, amongst others a privy, which was added to the house from outside. In some sagas it appears that the saga writer thought that one had to go outside to use a privy. In *The Saga of the People of Laxardal*, Kjartan barricades

*The Society of the Sagas of Icelanders*   67

the farm at Sælingsdalstunga, where Gudrun and Bolli live, and "in this way he forced them to shit inside for three days" (Chapter 47; author's translation). Unsurprisingly, it is considered a serious degradation, when the armed Kjartan prevents them from going outside to the privy, so that they have to defecate inside.

The picture on p. 65 shows a cross section of the main room at Stöng, which gives an impression of how the building is believed to have been constructed. It had a skeleton of timber on which the roof rested and was built of turf and stones. In *Njal's Saga*, Gunnar's farm is described almost as a fortress, but the roof can be winched off, which is what Gunnar's enemies do by attaching ropes around the ends of the roof beams and then turning them. The smoke went out through the louver in the roof. Some sagas relate how cunning inhabitants during a search burn wet and moist firewood, filling the room with smoke and forcing the ransackers to leave the house in a hurry. In addition to the living room, there was an extra room and various rooms for storing foodstuff. In *The Saga of the People of Eyri*, mention is made of a room full of dried fish (Chapter 53). The room had narrow benches in contrast to the broader sleeping quarters in the main living room. Beds could also be constructed as alcoves, cubicles, where one could sleep. Egil locks himself into his alcove when he wishes to die (Chapter 79).

The sagas relate that the farmer sat in the high-seat, while the distinguished guests sat on a bench opposite him. Sometimes, the guest is placed in a seat of honor. The benches are often referred to as the "upper" and "lower" benches. The women sat on the cross-bench. The seating arrangements can quickly become a source of conflict. When Kjartan marries Hrefna, he makes it clear that she is to sit in the seat of honor, instead of Gudrun, who had always "enjoyed the privilege of sitting in the seat of honour at Hjardarholt as elsewhere" (Chapter 46). In *The Saga of the People of Ljosavatn*, a man humorously threatens Gudmund the Powerful to vacate the seat of honor where he is accustomed to sit:

> And when the tables were set, Ofeig put his fist on the table and said, "How big does that fist seem to you, Gudmund?" "Big," he said. "Do you suppose there is any strength in it?" asked Ofeig. "I certainly do," said Gudmund. "Do you think it would deliver much of a blow?" asked Ofeig. "Quite a blow," Gudmund answered. "Do you think it might do any damage?" said Ofeig. "Broken bones or a deathblow," Gudmund answered. "How would such an end appeal to you?" asked Ofeig. "Not much at all, and I wouldn't choose it," said Gudmund. Ofeig said, "Then don't sit in my place." "As you wish," said Gudmund, and he sat to one side.
>
> (Chapter 21)

The saga writers did not always imagine that the benches were placed against the wall. When Gest kills Styr, he walks between the bench and the wall, so that he

68　*The Sagas of Icelanders*

can attack Styr from behind (*The Saga of the Slayings on the Heath*, Chapter 9). The high-seat pillars may have been pillars on each side of the high-seat. Several texts mention that the settlers brought the pillars with them from Norway and threw them into the sea, when they approached Iceland, in order to settle where they drifted ashore (cf. Thorolf Moster-beard in *The Saga of the People of Eyri*, Chapter 4). However, no high-seat pillars have been found in archaeological excavations, and so it has not been possible to ascertain the location of either the high-seat or seat of honor.

### Ships

Sailing and navigation are vital for the Icelanders in the sagas. It is rare to find a saga or a *þáttr* that does not mention one or more ships or people who journey abroad or return home. The heroes travel between Iceland and Norway, and they sail to Ireland, the British Isles, the Baltic countries, and they undertake exploratory journeys to Greenland in order to settle and from there farther west: to Helluland, Markland, and finally Vinland. They sail abroad to trade and harry, although the latter is toned down in the sagas of Icelanders compared to the sagas of ancient times, and they return with wealth and honor. Pleasure is not their motivation for sailing. *The Saga of the Sworn Brothers* tells of a crew tired of being at sea after having sailed from Norway to Iceland (Chapter 25), and if the orientation fails and one drifts off course, it can happen that an uprising threatens among the crew, as happens in *The Saga of the People of Laxardal* (Chapter 21). Sailing is a necessity.

The saga writers' descriptions provide insight into a maritime and masculine world, to which women have access only as passive passengers. Only once, in *Kormak's saga*, does a woman take over steering a ship, but that is only because Kormak has caused her husband to lose consciousness by hitting him with the tiller. The woman has no control over the ship and steers directly into the side of Kormak's ship, so that it capsizes (Chapter 25).

The sagas tell about the manning of ships, conditions on board, and also the ships themselves. The ships were open and could be both rowed and sailed; some were oceangoing and strong, others were suitable for sailing in calm waters. But the saga writers were not archaeologists and did not know the ships of the past, which is why many details in the sagas probably reflect (possibly erroneous) notions of ships in the thirteenth and fourteenth centuries. Accordingly, a *kuggi* has made its way into several sagas; this ship was used by the North European Hanseatic cities in the Middle Ages and has nothing to do with the Viking Age. Nonetheless, the sagas' accounts of navigation and life at sea provide a vivid picture of this aspect of the world in the Saga Age. *Egil's Saga* (Chapter 17) relates that Thorolf equips a ship for trading goods in England. In *The Tale of Audun from the Westfjords*, Audun hauls a polar bear across the Atlantic Ocean, from Greenland to Denmark. At the end of *The Saga of Hallfred the Troublesome Poet*, Hallfred is struck by a spear and receives a mortal

The Society of the Sagas of Icelanders 69

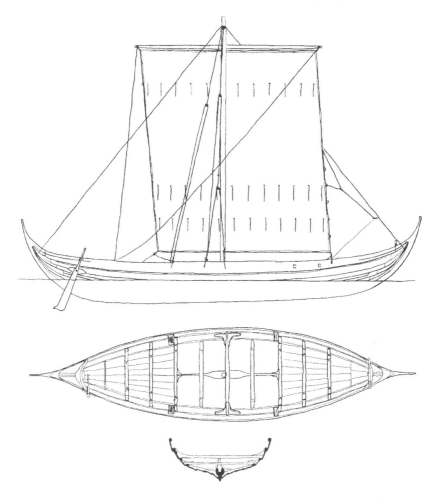

*Figure 13.4* A *byrðingr* (cargo ship). Skuldelev 3. Soren Nielsen, The Viking Ship Museum, Roskilde.

wound. In *Eirik the Red's Saga* (Chapter 13), a ship is infested with maggots or shipworms while at sea. On the sinking ship, the men have to decide who is permitted to get into the lifeboat and who must go down with the ship. In *The Saga of the Sworn Brothers* (Chapter 20), they have to bail water out of the ship on their way to Greenland. Sometimes conflicts arise on board, for example, when Grettir the Strong refuses to take equal part with the others in working on a ship:

> Grettir made himself a place to sleep under the ship's boat and refused to leave it, neither to bail out the ship nor turn the sails, nor do any of the tasks on board he was supposed to share with the rest of the crew. Nor would he

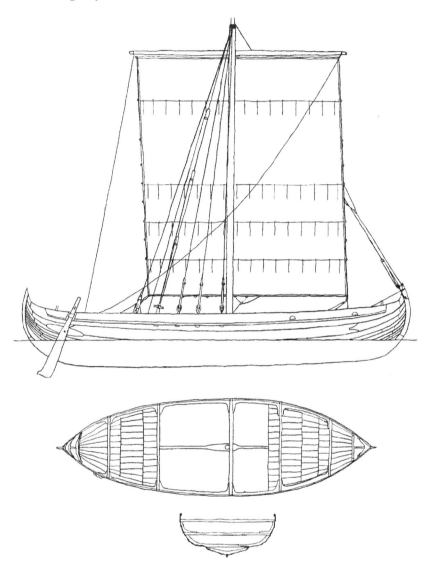

*Figure 13.5* A *knǫrr* (cargo ship). Skuldelev 1. Soren Nielsen, The Viking Ship Museum, Roskilde.

pay them to be relieved of his duties. They sailed south around Reykjanes and then along the south of Iceland, and when they lost sight of land they ran into strong breaking waves. The ship tended to leak and could hardly stand up to the breakers, and the crew were drenched. Grettir kept making *lampoons* about them, which infuriated them. One day when it was both windy and cold, the crew called out to Grettir and told him to pull his weight – "Our fingers

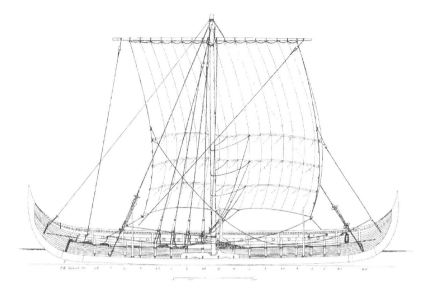

*Figure 13.6* A *karfi* (galley). The Gokstad ship. Saga Forlag, Reykjavík.

are frozen to the bone." Grettir looked up and said: "What luck if every layabout's fingers would shrivel up and drop off. They could not get him to work, but disliked his behaviour all the more and said they would make him pay for all the lampoons and offences he had made. "You'd much rather stroke Bard's wife's belly with your hands than do your duties on board," they said. "We won't stand for it." The weather grew steadily worse and the crew had to bail the ship out day and night, and they started threatening Grettir.

(Chapter 17)

The situation on board is tense, and, of course, it does not help that Grettir recites mocking verses, while the others slog away in order to survive.

The sagas tell of distress at sea and shipwrecks. In *The Saga of Finnbogi the Mighty* (Chapter 8), the young Finnbogi rescues the survivors of a crew in distress at sea, who have lit a fire on their ship to get help. Eirik the Red's son Leif gets his byname, the Lucky, for rescuing a crew in distress at sea (*Eirik the Red's Saga*, Chapter 5). And in *The Saga of the People of Floi*, a young boy is washed overboard by an enormous wave, and even though he is washed on board again, he subsequently dies, to his father's grief. In *The Saga of the People of Laxardal*, things also go wrong. Gudrun's fourth husband, Thorkel, is shipwrecked on Breidafjord on his way home from Norway. The boat is struck by a squall, capsizes, and Thorkel and all the men on board are drowned. When Gudrun goes to church in the evening, she sees a dead man, who briefly says

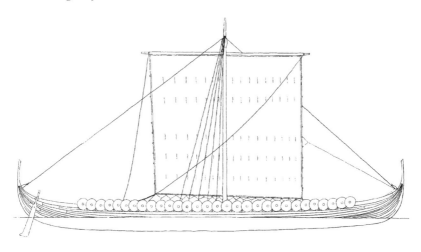

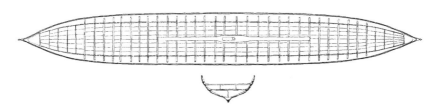

*Figure 13.7* A *skeið* (warship). Skuldelev 2. Soren Nielsen, The Viking Ship Museum, Roskilde.

"News of great moment, Gudrun" (Chapter 76). By the church, she sees Thorkel and his men with sea water dripping from their clothes, and she believes that Thorkel has come home. It is not until later that she understands that what she saw were the drowned men.

Many of the descriptions seem quite realistic, although this is not always the case. According to *Orm Storolfsson's Tale* (*Orms þáttr Stórólfssonar*) it took sixty men to lift the mast of Olaf Tryggvason's legendary ship, The Long Serpent—and yet Orm Storolfsson was so strong, that he could take three steps while holding the mast all by himself.

The many designations for types of ships reflect the large role played by ships and sailing in the Saga Age and in the world of the saga writers. In manuscripts of Snorri's *Edda*, there is an enumeration, in which Snorri reels off ship designations in four stanzas, followed by six stanzas with designations of ship

*The Society of the Sagas of Icelanders* 73

equipment and accessories. Snorri's *Edda* was written at the same time as many of the sagas of Icelanders.

Today's knowledge of the ships from the Saga Age does not come from the sagas, but rather archaeological finds, primarily in Roskilde Fjord by Skuldelev, Denmark. The archaeological finds show that the vessels of the Saga Age— or the Viking Age—were light; their draft was not deep, and they could be pulled ashore without difficulty. The warships were large, long, and slender ships, which could be both sailed and rowed. Royal ships like the famous Long Serpent, which is mentioned in the sagas, often had more than thirty oarsmen. According to the Norwegian kings' sagas, *Heimskringla*, The Long Serpent was no less than 43 meters long. In the Viking Ship Museum in Roskilde, Denmark, there is a reconstruction of a warship: the longship Skuldelev 2, "The Seahorse," which is thirty meters long—thirteen meters shorter than the alleged length of Olaf's ship.

### The Most Common Ship Designations

The word *ferja* ("ferry") is the name of a smaller cargo vessel, which is not oceanworthy. The word *skúta* designates a small, light ship. One of the most common types of ships in the sagas of Icelanders is the *knǫrr*, which is a strong, oceangoing cargo ship. The *byrðingr* is another cargo ship, which was suitable for sailing along the coast. In comparison to the warships, the cargo ships and the trading ships were broader, deeper, and shorter. The warships were long and slender and could sail at a high speed. A "longship" is a general term for large warships with many oars. A *skeið* is a large, narrow, and fast oceangoing warship. A *snekki* is a small longship, smaller than a *skeið*. In *Egil's Saga*, mention is made of a *snekki* with room for twenty oarsmen. A *karfi* is a medium-sized ship, which was mainly propelled by oars. There is uncertainty about this type of ship, but it is believed to have been smaller and more slender than a *knǫrr*. *Egil's Saga* mentions a *karfi*, which is rowed by twelve men on each side (Chapter 36), but in the same saga there is also mention of a *karfi* that is rowed by six men on each side (Chapter 58). In *The Saga of Grettir the Strong*, however, mention is made of a large *karfi* with thirty-two oarsmen (Chapter 18). Finally, the *dreki* ("dragon"), is a particularly distinguished warship with one or more dragon-heads on the bow. The name of Olaf Tryggvason's ship, The Long Serpent, does not reveal more than that it was an especially long example of this particular type of ship, because the Old Norse/Icelandic word *ormr* means both serpent and dragon.

# 14 The Sagas of Icelanders. A Survey

This chapter presents in alphabetical order (according to their titles in *The Complete Sagas of Icelanders*) a short survey of the content, dating, and transmission of the individual sagas.

### Bard's Saga (*Bárðar saga Snæfellsáss*)

Believed to have been written in 1350–1380 belongs to the late medieval period. This unusual saga, which takes place on Snæfellsnes in western Iceland during the Age of Settlement, may be characterized as a trolls' saga; accordingly, it differs from most of the other sagas of Icelanders. The protagonist Bard is of mixed descent: on his mother's side, he is descended from humans, but on his father's side, from trolls and giants. In addition, there are trolls in the Icelandic landscape—they dwell in caves, eat human flesh, and fight. The saga falls into two parts; the first part focuses primarily on Bard, and the other on his son Gest. Bard's daughter Helga plays an important role in both parts of the saga. The saga includes loosely connected episodes, while Bard often remains in the background after leaving the human world and killing his nephews. Subsequently, he appears as a local guardian spirit.

The saga relates that Bard is raised by the giant Dofri in Norway, whom one also meets in *The Saga of the People of Kjalarnes*. When Bard dreams that a man from whom the great missionary King Olaf the Saint is descended will visit Dofri's cave, he departs with Dofri's daughter, whom he has married. Bard's wife dies, and he emigrates to Iceland with their daughters. While playing with her male cousins, Helga steps out onto an icefloe and drifts off to Greenland, where she becomes the lover of the Icelander Skeggi who is married. When Helga and Skeggi return to Iceland, Bard brings her home against her will. After this, she withdraws from human beings and lives mostly in caves. Bard visits Helga's lover Skeggi, and impregnates his daughter. The child, Gest, is fostered by Helga. Gest helps two brothers, Thord and Thorvald, free a girl, who has been taken captive by trolls, and later follows them to Norway. On a voyage to Greenland, during which Odin appears and preaches paganism, Gest breaks

DOI: 10.4324/9781003499923-14

open the grave mound of an awe-inspiring mound-dweller. In the fight against the mound-dweller, Gest realizes that his father's heathen powers are insufficient and invokes the Christian God, promising to be baptized. Toward the end of the saga, Gest is baptized, but Bard appears in a dream, reproaches him for abandoning the old faith, and pokes at his eyes so hard that they burst. Gest dies the next day in his baptismal clothes.

The saga was composed by a learned and well-read saga writer. He used information from the *Book of Settlements*, theological texts, and *The Great Saga of Olaf Tryggvason* (*Óláfs saga Tryggvasonar en mesta*). The saga is preserved in five medieval fragments, the oldest of which dates to around 1390–1425 (AM 564 a 4to). It is also extant in a number of late copies, the most important of which are AM 158 fol. and AM 486 4to, both from the seventeenth century.

### Egil's saga (*Egils saga Skalla-Grímssonar*)

One of the longest sagas has been dated to around 1230 and is believed to be one of the oldest sagas of Icelanders. Snorri Sturluson (1179–1241) has been suggested as the author by several scholars. The saga may be divided into two parts: the first revolves around Egil's ancestors in Norway, while the second deals with Egil. In the beginning, one of the themes of the saga is introduced, that of a freeman's conflict with royal power. The saga is unambiguous in its criticism of Norwegian royal power. The family emigrates to Iceland because of Harald Fair-hair's tyranny and settles in Borgarfjord. The saga follows Egil throughout his long life: as a three-year-old, composing his first verse; as a seven-year-old, committing his first killing; as a twelve-year-old, sailing abroad for the first time; and as an old man, stumbling around by the fire. While abroad and in his dealings with the Norwegian king, Egil is stubborn and intractable, but at home in Iceland he is (generally) peaceful. Egil and the royal couple, Eirik Blood-axe and Gunnhild, are lifelong mortal enemies. Egil is tough and avaricious; he knows runes and magic; he commits brutal and bestial acts of violence. At the same time, however, he is faithful and sensitive, as is evident in his long poems. His poetry sometimes becomes a matter of life and death; the first time, when he composes *Head Ransom* (*Hǫfuðlausn*) for Eirik Blood-axe and keeps his own head as a reward for the poem; and a second time, when he has lost his son Bodvar and locked himself inside his alcove to die, but is tricked by his daughter Thorgerd into composing a memorial poem, *Loss of Sons* (*Sonatorrek*), about his loss, and regains his zest for life through poetry.

The saga is preserved in three redactions (A-redaction in Möðruvallabók, AM 132 fol. ca. 1350; B-redaction primarily in the Wolfenbüttel codex (Herzog August Bibliothek MS 9.10. Aug. 4to); and C in the so-called Ketilsbækur, AM 462 4to and AM 453 4to, which differ with regard to Egil's poetry and religion. Only the C-redaction of the saga, believed to have been written in the late Middle Ages, contains both *Head Ransom* and *Loss of Sons*. The A-redaction has

*Figure 14.1* The beginning of *Eirik the Red's Saga* in Hauksbók (right page). The redaction of the saga in this manuscript is abridged. AM 544 4to (ca. 1300), The Arnamagnæan Collection, University of Copenhagen. Photo: Suzanne Reitz.

the fullest prose text and most of Egil's situational verses, but does not include *Head Ransom* and *Loss of Sons*, and adds *Arinbjorn's Poem* at the end of the saga. The B-redaction does not contain *Loss of Sons*, only *Head Ransom*. The theta-fragment of *Egil's Saga* from ca. 1250 (AM 162 A θ fol.) is the oldest fragment of a saga of Icelanders.

### *Eirik the Red's Saga* (*Eiríks saga rauða*)

Believed to have been written at the beginning of the thirteenth century, it is considered as one of the oldest sagas of Icelanders. The saga is introduced by a chapter, the content of which is also found in *The Saga of the People of Laxardal* and the *Book of Settlements*. Otherwise, the saga is partly based on *The Saga of the Greenlanders*. In comparison with this saga, *Eirik the Red's Saga* appears to a higher degree as a literary composition. The saga confirms historical facts, notably the discovery in around 1960 by Helge Ingstad and Anne Stine Ingstad of a Viking dwelling in L'Anse aux Meadows, Newfoundland, Canada, dating to around 1000.

While *The Saga of the Greenlanders* tells of seven voyages outside of the known world (to Greenland and Vinland), *Eirik the Red's Saga* tells of four. Eirik the Red sails to Greenland after being outlawed in Iceland. One of his sons, Leif, is asked by the Norwegian king, Olaf Tryggvason, to Christianize the people in

Greenland. Leif drifts off course and accidentally discovers some lands, where he takes note of the vegetation before he sails back to Greenland. On his way back, he rescues a crew in distress at sea near Greenland, and when he reaches his destination, he successfully introduces Christianity in Greenland. The third time, Eirik's son Thorstein sets sail, but the crew is storm-tossed at sea and fails to reach the destination. Exhausted, the crew returns, and Thorstein dies shortly after. The crew of the fourth and final voyage, led by Karlsefni and Snorri, successfully finds the New World, where they encounter *skrælingjar* (native Americans), with whom they trade. The Norsemen and the *skrælingjar* clash in battle, and the Norsemen depart. On their voyage, they pass *Einfætingaland* ("Land of the one-legged") and encounter one-legged inhabitants. They capture two children, whom they baptize and teach the Norse language. Karlsefni, Snorri, and their colleagues make it back, but not everyone is so lucky. One ship is infested with shipworms and sinks with nearly all aboard, while another ship veers off course. Karl and his wife Gudrid are among the survivors, and in Vinland, Gudrid has given birth to a boy, Snorri. The saga concludes by noting that several bishops are descendants of Snorri. It should be noted that Gudrid embarks on a pilgrimage to Rome, bridging Christianity and the new world. She is the most widely-traveled person not only in the sagas of Icelanders but also in the Middle Ages.

In comparison to *The Saga of the Greenlanders*, the boundary between Christianity and paganism is emphasized in *Eirik the Red's Saga*. Eirik is to a higher degree portrayed as a heathen. He refuses to accept the Christian faith and therefore lives apart from his wife Thjodhild. The Greenlanders also appear heathen to a higher degree: a seeress travels from farm to farm with her prophecies, and during the last journey to Vinland, a heathen invokes Thor; subsequently a beached whale appears, which turns out to be poisonous.

The saga is preserved in two medieval manuscripts, Hauksbók (AM 544 4to, ca. 1300) and Skálholtsbók (AM 577 4to, ca. 1420–1450), which is believed to be the better text.


### Gisli Sursson's Saga (*Gísla saga Súrssonar*)

Generally dated to around 1250, it belongs to the middle group of the sagas of Icelanders. The saga, which features an outlaw as its protagonist, takes place in the Westfjords. It is famous for its composition and may be divided into two parts. The first part takes place in Norway, and the second in Iceland. The four siblings Thordis, Thorkel, Gisli, and Ari are raised in Norway. Thordis is beautiful, and there are rumors that she has been seduced by Bard, Thorkel's friend. The father is opposed to this affair, and so Gisli kills Bard, which leads to a breach in the relationship among the brothers. Gisli kills yet another man, who has seduced Thordis, and then also a suitor, before the family settles in Iceland. In Iceland, Thordis marries Thorgrim, a friend of Thorkel. Gisli marries Aud, sister of Vestein, a close friend of Gisli's, and finally Thorkel marries Asgerd.

78   *The Sagas of Icelanders*

The four men's attempt at sworn brotherhood collapses when Thorgrim refuses to commit to Vestein. While Vestein is abroad, a love affair between Thorkel's wife Asgerd and Vestein is revealed, and it becomes clear that Gisli's wife Aud previously had a relationship with Thorgrim. When Vestein returns, Gisli tries to warn him, but his warning comes too late. Vestein is killed by an unknown man, although it is clear that Thorkel and Thorgrim are behind the murder. Taking revenge, Gisli kills his brother-in-law Thorgrim, while the latter is lying in bed with his wife, Gisli's sister. Thordis marries yet again, this time Bork, Thorgrim's brother. Later, Gisli recites a verse in which he reveals himself as the killer. Thordis mentions the verse to Bork, who has Gisli condemned to outlawry. The saga then describes Gisli's outlawry and his defense against his enemies, which culminates in his last battle, where he recites poems until his death. When Thordis hears of Gisli's death, she attacks Bork with a sword and declares herself divorced from him. Aud leaves Iceland, travels to Hedeby in Denmark, where she is baptized. She embarks on pilgrimage but dies en route.

The fatalism of the saga is among other things expressed in Gisli's dreams. But the saga is also a story of Gisli's development: at first, Gisli is presented as a heathen, not sparing anyone to save himself. In his dreams, he is visited by two dream-women, one good and one evil. The good dream-woman instructs him to be kind to the blind, lame, poor, and troubled, and to turn away from the old faith. Later in the saga, Gisli enables a slave and his companions to buy their freedom, thereby mirroring the efforts of humble people, who strive to help him. In the course of events, Gisli's conduct becomes increasingly more Christian.

The saga is transmitted in a shorter and a longer redaction. The longer redaction, which includes mention of supernatural elements in the beginning, is not preserved in its entirety. Scholars lean toward the opinion that the shorter redaction, which is preserved in AM 556 a 4to (ca. 1475–1500) is the older, but this is uncertain. A fragment (AM 445 c I 4to) indicates the existence of a third redaction.

### Gold-Thorir's Saga (*Gull-Þóris saga*)

Also called "The Saga of the People of Thorskafjord" (*Þorskfirðinga saga*), it dates to around 1350 and therefore belongs to the late medieval period. Set early in the Age of Settlement before 930, it stands out as the sole saga of Icelanders featuring a dragon in Iceland. The first part of the saga is set in Norway; the second part in Thorskafjord in the Westfjords.

The saga follows the young Gold-Thorir on his adventures in Norway. He attempts to open a burial mound, but is warned in a dream by the mound-dweller, who reveals that they are relatives. In return, Gold-Thorir receives armor with magical powers and a large portion of the gold and silver. He complains that it is insufficient, and the mound-dweller curses him: only late will Gold-Thorir tire of wealth. The mound-dweller informs Gold-Thorir about a treasure guarded by dragons and gives him a magic potion with strict instructions on how to

The Sagas of Icelanders. A Survey    79

consume it. Gold-Thorir accepts the magic potion but ignores the instructions. Along with his companions, he crosses a mighty waterfall, defeats the dragons in a cave north of Norway, and wins their treasure. The same dragons appear in *Halfdan Eysteinsson's Saga* (*Hálfdanar saga Eysteinssonar*), a saga of ancient times, where three sinister persons, Valr, Kǫttr, and Kisi, transform themselves into dragons and guard a treasure in a waterfall until Gold-Thorir arrives. When Gold-Thorir divides the dragon treasure, the curse is recalled by the reader. Gold-Thorir takes the largest share and locks it up in two chests. Back in Iceland, quarrels arise because the father of one of the companions considers the division to be unfair. Conflicts in the fjord escalate over rights to a stranded whale, pasture, and lost sheep. Many people get involved, including two women skilled in magic, Thurid drikkin ("dungcheek") and Kerling. Eventually, the two conflicting parties reconcile. Later, however, the mound-dweller's curse takes effect: Gold-Thorir becomes evil and harsh and ultimately transforms himself into a dragon, lying on his chests of gold.

The saga is preserved in a manuscript from ca. 1400 (AM 561 4to). The text of some of the leaves has been scraped off, and editors of the saga have filled in the missing text from younger nineteenth-century manuscripts.

### Hen-Thorir's Saga (*Hænsa-Þóris saga*)

Dated to around 1250–1270, it belongs to the middle period and is set in the area around Borgarfjord in western Iceland. This short saga, devoid of illusoriness, is believed to be based on historical events, since some of them are mentioned in Ari's *Book of Icelanders*. The protagonist, Hen-Thorir, is an unscrupulous upstart who amasses wealth by trading other people's goods. Despite his wealth, he remains unpopular. During a hard winter with famine, Hen-Thorir, with ample supplies, refuses to sell anything to Blund-Ketil, despite generous offers. Eventually, Blund-Ketil leaves money and takes the needed hay. Hen-Thorir accuses him of theft after having bribed supporters. At the assembly, a Norwegian accidentally kills Arngrim, the chieftain's son fostered by Hen-Thorir. Hen-Thorir takes advantage of the incident to manipulate the men to burn Blund-Ketil and his household in their house. Hen-Thorir is killed, and the arsonists are exiled. The burning's repercussions in the local community are manifold and bloody and make the judgment seem anticlimactic.

A fifteenth-century fragment of the saga exists (AM 162 G fol.), but otherwise, it is preserved only in young paper manuscripts derived from a lost medieval manuscript.

### Killer-Glum's Saga (*Víga-Glúms saga*)

Dated to ca. 1270–1280, it belongs to the middle period. The saga is set in tenth-century Eyjafjord in northern Iceland. The introductory chapters tell of

80   *The Sagas of Icelanders*

the heroic deeds of Killer-Glum's father in Norway. Thereafter the saga focuses on Killer-Glum in his youth a coal-biter. He proves his worth when he kills a berserk in Norway at the age of fifteen. Back in Iceland, through his killing and resorting to the law, he protects his mother against greedy family members. The killing results in a number of conflicts and culminates in a battle, where Killer-Glum commits a killing, which he manages to blame on a twelve-year old, who is outlawed. Glum boasts of the killing in a verse, for which reason the case is reopened. He attempts to avoid punishment by swearing an ambiguous oath, but is forced to leave his farm. He then lives in seclusion, but despite his attempts at revenge, he is unable to regain his powerful position. Toward the end of the saga, Glum is baptized and dies shortly after. Earlier, Glum had worshiped Frey, with whom he had an ambiguous relationship; indeed, it may be because of a sacrifice to Frey that Glum had to leave his farm.

Most of Chapter 16 bears a strong resemblance to Chapter 26 in *The Saga of the People of Reykjadal and of Killer-Skuta*. It is uncertain whether *Killer-Glum's saga* borrowed from *The Saga of the People of Reykjadal and of Killer-Skuta* or vice versa, though most scholars lean toward the former. Some of Killer-Glum's verses are preserved in Snorri's *Edda*.

The saga is preserved completely only in a single medieval manuscript, Möðruvallabók (AM 132 fol., ca. 1350). Medieval fragments survive of a longer redaction (AM 445 c I 4to and AM 564 a 4to, ca. 1390–1425), but this redaction has not been preserved in its entirety.

### Kormak's Saga (*Kormáks saga*)

Dated to the first half of the thirteenth century, it belongs to the oldest group of sagas. It is a skald saga revolving around the maladapted skald Kormak, whose love life is messy and complicated.

At his first glimpse of Steingerd's feet peeking out from under a door, Kormak falls deeply in love. Despite his forceful wooing, he is never betrothed to her. Steingerd is also courted by Odd, whom Kormak kills. When Kormak drives Odd's mother, the prophetess Thordis, from her farm, she places a curse on Kormak that he will never marry Steingerd. Shortly afterward, Kormak has the opportunity to marry her but does not show up at the wedding. According to the saga, this is a result of magic—but his unfulfilled love inspires much poetry. Steingerd is unwillingly married to Bersi, and Kormak reproaches her for that. Kormak maims Bersi, whereafter Steingerd divorces him. Later, she is willingly married to Thorvald Tintein, but Kormak does not give up, as he is always thinking of Steingerd. He composes verses during a terrible storm at sea (like Frithiof in *The Saga of Frithiof the Bold* (*Friðþjófs saga frœkna*). When the prophetess Thordis later tries to recant the curse, so that Kormak can marry Steingerd, it is his own fault that it does not happen. After rescuing Steingerd from Vikings multiple times, Thorvald Tintein agrees to their marriage, but Kormak refuses due to

*Figure 14.2 Njal's Saga* (Reykjabók). The pages show a passage from the judicial settlement after the burning of Bergthorshvol, the beginning of Chapter 144 ("Now Asgrim sent …"). AM 468 4to (ca. 1300–1325), The Arnamagnæan Collection, University of Copenhagen. Photo: Suzanne Reitz.

the curse. Shortly afterward, Kormak is mortally wounded in Scotland and dies while reciting a verse about Steingerd.

Kormak is a historical skald, who lived in the eleventh century. Some of his verses are preserved in Snorri's *Edda*, but these verses, which are considered authentic, are not included in the saga. The saga writer is not interested in the historical Kormak's career as a court poet. The description of the lovesick skald is unique among the sagas of Icelanders, which has led scholars to speculate that it may have been inspired by southern European troubadour poetry and the story about Tristan and Isolde.

The saga is preserved in its entirety only in Möðruvallabók (AM 132 fol., ca. 1350).

### *Njal's Saga (Brennu-Njáls saga)*

Dated to the late thirteenth century, it belongs to the middle period. It is the longest saga of Icelanders and is renowned for its artistic and well-motivated composition. The saga writer was well-versed in existing saga literature and foreign works, including theological, courtly, and historiographic texts. The protagonists are the close friends Gunnar and Njal and their quarrelsome wives Hallgerd and Bergthora. In contrast to their wives, Gunnar and Njal seek peace

82   *The Sagas of Icelanders*

and forgiveness. Nonetheless, both meet tragic ends: Gunnar is attacked on his farm and betrayed by Hallgerd, while Njal is burned in his home with his household. The saga can be divided into three parts: the first centers on Gunnar (with a prelude about Unn's and Hallgerd's marriages), the second on Njal, and the third on the conflict and settlement after the burning of Bergthorshvol. The saga demonstrates how individual conflicts can challenge the entire legal system and bring Icelandic society to the brink of civil war twice: first, when armed heathens and Christians ride to the Althing before the introduction of Christianity, and second, after the burning. The major event in the saga is the introduction of Christianity, which is detailed in *The Tale about Christianity* (*Kristni þáttr*). The final solution is Christian forgiveness, as exemplified by Flosi, the leader of the burners, and Njal's son-in-law, Kari, who after a long time and a pilgrimage wholeheartedly reach a settlement and are reconciled when Kari marries Hildigunn, the widow of Njal's sons' innocent victim Hoskuld.

The saga is preserved in about sixty manuscripts; of these twenty-one are from the Middle Ages. The oldest date from ca. 1300, of which three are almost complete: Reykjabók (AM 468 4to, ca. 1300–1325), considered the best manuscript from a text-critical point of view; Kálfalækjarbók (AM 133 fol., ca. 1350); and Gráskinna (GKS 2870 4to, ca. 1300).

### Olkofri's Saga (*Qlkofra saga*)

Also known as *The Tale about Olkofri* (*Qlkofra þáttr*), it is a short saga, believed to have been written in the middle period, during the mid-thirteenth century. It is set in southwestern Iceland, primarily at the Althing. The protagonist of the saga is Thorhal, known as Olkofri, because of his sale of ale and his clothing. Olkofri is no hero: he is old, small, and ugly. When he burns coal, he accidentally burns down a forest owned by six chieftains. They band together to have Olkofri outlawed due to his negligence. At the assembly, Olkofri receives help from Broddi Bjarnason and Thorstein Sidu-Hallsson, and Olkofri almost breaks down in tears for joy. With his pitiful behavior, Olkofri manages to trick the chieftains into accepting monetary compensation instead of sentencing him to outlawry. Olkofri is then allowed to pick the person, who is to settle the matter. They expect him to pick someone from their group, but instead he chooses Broddi and Thorstein, who ask him to pay only a slight symbolic compensation. When the chieftains complain, Broddi trounces them verbally and accuses them of unmanly behavior. Nonetheless, Broddi becomes reconciled with one of the chieftains and rides with him from the assembly.

This brief saga is a satirical commentary on the powerful chieftains' avarice and the corruption of the entire legal system. It shares thematic similarities with *The Saga of the Confederates*, and the eddic poem *Loki's Quarrel* (*Lokasenna*), where Loki accuses the assembled gods of *níð*.

The saga is preserved in Möðruvallabók (AM 132 fol., ca. 1350).

*The Sagas of Icelanders. A Survey* 83

### The Saga of Bjorn, Champion of the Hitardal People (*Bjarnar saga Hítdœlakappa*)

It is a skald saga belonging to the oldest period and may be dated to 1215–1230. The saga takes place primarily in the western part of Iceland and depicts a skald's lifelong unhappy love for a woman, a theme it shares with other skald sagas.

The protagonists are the rivals Bjorn Arngeirsson and Thord Kolbeinsson, both skalds. Bjorn and Oddny, who are in love, are betrothed before he leaves for Norway; if he does not return in three years, her father can marry her to another man. While Bjorn is in the retinue of Earl Eirik, Thord arrives, and the two treat each other well despite previous disagreements. Thord convinces Bjorn to let him visit Oddny to confirm her betrothal to Bjorn. While Bjorn is in Garðaríki (Russia), where he performs a heroic deed by which he earns his byname, Thord sails to Iceland, claims that Bjorn has died, and marries Oddny. After several adventures abroad (among others at the court of Canute the Great in England, where he kills a dragon; and with King Olaf, who makes him end his Viking raids), he returns to Iceland. During the winter, Bjorn stays with Thord and Oddny. Although Bjorn and Thord do not physically attack each other, they mock each other in verses. In one verse, Bjorn reveals that during the winter he and Oddny had an affair, and several years later he recognizes himself in Oddny's son Kolli. Thord and Bjorn's mocking verses escalate, despite other men's attempts to stop them through legal means. The conflict leads to violence and attacks on Bjorn by Thord, when Bjorn carves a scorn-figure, showing Thord in a homosexual act. In the final battle, where Bjorn dies, he is also severely attacked by his and Oddny's son Kolli. When Bjorn reveals that he is Kolli's father, Kolli immediately stops. Thord cuts off Bjorn's head, and throws it to Bjorn's mother with a derisive remark. When Oddny hears what has happened, she pines away with grief and dies.

The saga shares themes with *The Saga of the People of Laxardal*, *The Saga of Gunnlaug Serpent-Tongue*, and *The Saga of Thorstein the White* which is believed to have inspired it along with *The Saga of the People of Eyri*.

The transmission of the saga is problematic: only one fragment of the saga from the Middle Ages (AM 162 F fol., ca. 1350–1400) has been preserved, and in the younger manuscripts, where it is preserved more fully, the first five chapters are missing, which editors have taken from a tale about Bjorn in *The Great Saga of Saint Olaf*. It has been impossible to reconstruct the second lacuna in the saga.

### The Saga of Droplaug's Sons (*Droplaugarsona saga*)

It is considered to be among the oldest sagas of Icelanders and believed to have been recorded in the first half of the thirteenth century. The saga is set in the

*Figure 14.3* Möðruvallabók is the largest manuscript containing sagas of Icelanders. It includes eleven sagas of Icelanders and one *þáttr*. AM 132 fol. (ca. 1350), The Árni Magnússon Institute for Icelandic Studies, Reykjavík Photo: Jóhanna Ólafsdóttir.

eastern part of Iceland and follows four generations of the same family. Some passages give the impression that the narrative was based on local tradition.

The saga begins with a short prehistory about Ketil Thrym, who marries a woman captured as a slave in the Hebrides. After buying her, he offers to bring her home to her family, but she chooses instead to go with him to Iceland. The saga then focuses on a conflict between Ketil's great-grandchildren, the two sons of Droplaug, Grim and Helgi, and the chieftain Helgi Asbjarnarson. The conflict begins, when Helgi Asbjarnarson's freed slave gossips that their mother does not have relations with only one man, and as a result they kill him. A different version is told in *The Saga of the People of Fljotsdal*, where Droplaug is provided with a fantastic prehistory. Later, Helgi Droplaugarson is probably also involved, when his stepfather Hallstein is killed. Because of this, he is outlawed and killed in an ambush. In the same battle, Grim is wounded, but recovers. The last part of the saga deals with Grim's avenging of his brother. He waits for the perfect moment and carries the revenge out at night with his brother's sword. Grim kills Helgi Asbjarnarson, who is lying in bed with his wife. Because of the killing Grim is also declared an outlaw, but manages to escape to Norway, where he dies after fighting a battle against an evil viking.

The murder scene in the marital bed is reminiscent of the nighttime murder in *Gisli Surssons's Saga*. The saga is believed to have served, to some extent, as a

The Sagas of Icelanders. A Survey   85

source for *Gisli Sursson's Saga*, *The Saga of the People of Laxardal*, *The Saga of the People of Fljotsdal*, and *The Saga of the People of Vopnafjord*.

The only complete text of the saga from the Middle Ages is found in Möðru-vallabók (AM 132 fol., ca. 1350), which is believed to be an abbreviated redaction of the original text. A small fragment, AM 162 C fol. (ca. 1420–1450), containing portions of Chapters 3 and 4, preserves a longer redaction, which is believed to be the original redaction.

### The Saga of Finnbogi the Mighty (*Finnboga saga ramma*)

Dated between 1300 and 1350, it is set primarily in northern Iceland and belongs to the younger period. The saga follows Finnbogi from beginning to end. Angry that his wife has given their daughter to a Norwegian without his knowledge, Finnbogi's father requests that her unborn child be exposed at the beginning of the saga. The child, Finnbogi, is saved and lovingly raised by a poor couple, who call him *Urðarkǫttr* ("Scree-cat"), because he was found in a scree. At the age of twelve, his kinship is revealed, and the father accepts him, even though he retains his strange name. As a young man, Finnbogi (alias Urdarkott), rescues the survivors on a ship in distress. The captain's name is Finnbogi, and he gives his rescuer his name and possessions before he dies from exhaustion. Finnbogi travels to Norway, where he displays remarkable strength and a good heart. He survives shipwrecks, kills bears, villains, a *blá-maðr* ("black man"), and finds a wife. In Greece, he becomes acquainted with Christianity and swears to be among the first to convert if Christianity reaches the north. The Byzantine emperor is impressed by his strength and nicknames him "the Mighty." Back in Iceland, where he is among the first to be baptized, Finnbogi is confronted with jealousy and conflicts, which lead to his banishment from the northern part of the country. He settles in Vididal, where his two young sons are killed, and his wife dies of grief. Though he longs for Norway, once he hears that Christianity has been introduced, his relative Thorgeir, chieftain of Ljosavatn, advises him to remain in Iceland. He remarries, but now gets into conflict with Ingimund's sons in Vatnsdal, especially the unyielding Jokul. One can also read about this feud in *The Saga of the People of Vatnsdal*, where the sympathy, however, is with Ingimund's sons. Eventually, Finnbogi becomes reconciled with his enemies, dies at an old age, and is buried at the church he built at Finnbogastadir.

The saga is preserved in a number of manuscripts, of which the two most important are Möðruvallabók (AM 132 fol., ca. 1350) and AM 510 4to (ca. 1550).

### The Saga of Grettir the Strong (*Grettis saga*)

One of the longest sagas of Icelanders, it belongs to the group of late medieval sagas. It has generally been dated to 1320–1350, but recently scholars have argued that it may have been written around 1400. The saga, which features an

86    *The Sagas of Icelanders*

outlaw as its protagonist, takes place in northern Iceland, in Norway, and on Drangey in Skagafjord. It follows Grettir Asmundarson from his sadistic tricks in boyhood to his adulthood as an outlaw. The saga may be divided into two parts: the first part deals with the time until Grettir's outlawry; the second with his nineteen years as an outlaw. During his life, Grettir fights revenants, trolls, berserks, a bear, opens a grave mound, has erotic experiences—and composes verses. It is no coincidence that he gets the reputation of being Iceland's strongest man. At the peak of his power, he frees Vatnsdal from the dangerous revenant Glam. As a result of the moonlit fight against Glam, Grettir becomes afraid of the dark, because the dying Glam places a curse on him: Grettir's actions shall bring him misfortune and loneliness. Shortly after their fight, Grettir visits Saint Olaf in Norway. The curse's impact becomes evident when Grettir swims in ice-cold water to fetch fire for his freezing friends but accidentally burns down a building housing travelers. The king offers Grettir a chance to clear himself by carrying a red-hot iron, but retracts it after Grettir kills a boy who mocks him. The burning also makes Grettir an outlaw in Iceland, where he roams from one hideout to another and becomes increasingly isolated. During his last three years as an outlaw, Grettir and his loyal younger brother barricade themselves on Drangey, a rocky island, which is hard to climb. After Grettir has spent nearly twenty years as an outlaw, his enemy Thorbjorn *ǫngul* ("hook") overcomes him with the help of magic. When the men arrive, Grettir is already close to death due to a severe leg infection. Nonetheless, his enemy kills him, severs his head, and salts it. Thorbjorn Hook gains no honor from his despicable killing of Grettir.

The last part of the saga, *The Tale about Spes* (*Spesar þáttr*), differs in style and content. It relates how Grettir's half-brother, Thorstein Dromund, avenges him in Constantinople. Thorstein has an affair with Spes, whose husband they betray. After many years of marriage, Thorstein and Spes repent and enter a monastery.

Despite its coarse humor and irony, the saga is a tragic account of a strong man's battle against inevitable fate. The saga writer was inspired by foreign and indigenous literature. Parallels have been found in Boccaccio's *Decameron*, in the Tristan legend, and in the Anglo-Saxon poem *Beowulf*, which, however, he cannot have known directly.

The saga is extant in one redaction, preserved in four medieval manuscripts, the oldest of which dates to the fifteenth century (AM 556 a 4to).

### *The Saga of Gunnar, the Fool of Keldugnup* (*Gunnars saga Keldugnúpsfífls*)

It is a short saga, which has been dated to the fifteenth century, that belongs to the youngest sagas of Icelanders. The saga begins and ends in southern Iceland. Gunnar, the fool of Keldugnup, is a typical coal-biter hanging out by the fire and subject to his father's contempt. He proves himself when he kills a man at

The Sagas of Icelanders. A Survey    87

a meeting in the region. After the killing, conflicts arise, and Gunnar travels to Norway. Before he departs, he is betrothed to Helga, a sister of his enemies. On his way into her house, Gunnar kills her two brothers, after which he enters and is greeted warmly by Helga. He sails off into a mystical darkness and comes to an unknown land with glaciers, trolls, and polar bears. Gunnar kills a polar bear, which seems to understand what he is saying, and several trolls, but he spares the troll-girl Fala, who in return supports him. In Norway, Gunnar's opponent is Earl Hakon. He demands that Gunnar fight a *blámaðr*, but Gunnar wins. Afterwards, he goes raiding and gets into a mortal battle with Vikings. He is reconciled with the earl, and back in Iceland, he marries Helga, though he still has to kill one of his old enemies, before the saga ends with the reconciliation of the two conflicting parties.

The saga shares motifs with the sagas of ancient times (e.g. the coal-biter and the helpful troll-girl). The saga writer appears to have known *Jokul Buason's Tale* (*Jǫkuls þáttr Búasonar*) and *The Saga of the People of Kjalarnes*. The saga writer does not attempt to make the story appear as a historical work.

The saga is preserved in a number of manuscripts, of which four are believed to be closest to the original: AM 496 4to (ca. 1640), AM 156 fol. (seventeenth century), AM 443 4to (seventeenth century), and AM 554 i 4to (seventeenth century).

### The Saga of Gunnlaug Serpent-Tongue
### (Gunnlaugs saga ormstungu)

It is believed to have been written ca. 1270–1280 in the middle period. The saga, which shares its plot with *The Saga of Bjorn, Champion of the Hitardal People*, *The Saga of the People of Laxardal*, and *The Saga of Thorstein the White*, is set in western Iceland, in Borgarfjord, but Gunnlaug also travels to the courts of kings and earls outside Iceland.

In the introduction to the saga, Helga's father has a dream, which predicts that two magnates will die because of his unborn daughter, and that she will be married to a third. He asks his wife to expose the baby girl, but the mother loves the girl and lets Egil Skallagrimsson's daughter Thorgerd raise her. Like most of the skald sagas, this saga also revolves around love. Gunnlaug is an uncontrollable and ambitious boy, who is nicknamed "Serpent-tongue" because of his derogatory remarks. At the age of twelve, he wants to go abroad, but he does not get permission from his father, and in defiance he moves to Borg, where he falls in love with Helga.

Six years later, he wants to go abroad again, but when the ship is ready to sail, he proposes to Helga. Neither Helga's father nor his own father is enthusiastic, but she is promised to him nonetheless and is to wait for him for three years. Gunnlaug visits one prince after another, where he recites his poems. But at the court of the Swedish king, where his countryman Hrafn is present, things go

88   *The Sagas of Icelanders*

wrong, when the two young men start quarreling and criticizing each other's poem in front of the king. Gunnlaug humiliates Hrafn, but Hrafn settles the score back in Iceland where he woos Helga and she is promised to him in marriage—against her will—unless Gunnlaug shows up at the wedding. Gunnlaug arrives in Borgarfjord on the day of the wedding, but his leg is out of joint, and for this reason he does not ride to the wedding. Hrafn and Gunnlaug have more clashes. They fight their last duel in Norway, where Hrafn uses one last dirty trick to kill Gunnlaug, and both die. Helga remarries, but never forgets Gunnlaug.

The saga is preserved in two medieval manuscripts: Holm perg 18 4to (ca. 1300–1350) and AM 557 4to (ca. 1420–1450), but the latter does not contain the entire saga.

### The Saga of Hallfred the Troublesome Poet
#### (*Hallfreðar saga vandræðaskálds*)

It is a skald saga, believed to date to the older period, around 1220. Hallfred is uncontrollable and fond of women. He falls in love with Kolfinna, but doesn't want to marry her when her father asks him to. Accordingly, the father arranges another match. Hallfred kisses Kolfinna in front of her betrothed and composes satirical verses about him. Hallfred is sent to Norway, where he enters the service of Olaf Tryggvason. He is hostile toward the new faith but agrees to be baptized by the king himself, who nicknames him *vandræðaskáld* ("troublesome poet"). Despite his baptism, Hallfred continues to praise the old gods, and the king complains about it. Some of Hallfred's verses deal with his reluctant conversion. It is only after a lengthy stay in Sweden, where he lives with a heathen woman and almost turns his back on Christianity, that Hallfred embraces the Christian faith wholeheartedly. The king visits Hallfred in his dreams and accuses him of apostasy, whereafter Hallfred returns and fully converts. Back in Iceland, Hallfred spends a night with Kolfinna, probably raping her, while composing mocking verses about her husband. It is only when Olaf warns Hallfred in a dream that his case against her husband is poor, the two rivals reconcile. Having learned that King Olaf is dead, Hallfred leaves Iceland in grief. On his way back to Iceland, the ship's boom hits him in the head during a storm, and he dies. His coffin drifts ashore in the Hebrides, where he receives a Christian burial.

Hallfred is a historical person mentioned as a court poet for earls and kings, including Olaf Tryggvason; several of his verses are transmitted in Snorri's *Edda* and the kings' sagas.

The saga is preserved in two redactions in manuscripts from the fourteenth century. One is incoherent and interwoven into *The Great Saga of Olaf Tryggvason* (e.g. in Flateyjarbók, GKS 1005 fol., ca. 1387–1395). The other redaction is found in Möðruvallabók (AM 132 fol. ca. 1350), which transmits the saga in its entirety and as a coherent text.

## The Saga of Havard of Isafjord (*Hávarðar saga Ísfirðings*)

It belongs to the late medieval period and dates to around 1330. It is set in tenth-century northwestern Iceland. Some scholars believe that the saga is a loose rewriting of a saga about Thorbjorn and Havard the Lame, mentioned in Sturla Þórðarson's redaction of the *Book of Settlements*. The saga writer subverts the common motif of a son avenging his father: instead, Havard's young son is killed by a local tyrant, and the saga tells the story of the aged father's revenge. Once a formidable viking, old Havard, upon hearing of his son's death, sighs loudly and takes to his bed, where he remains for three years, during which time his wife manages the farm. At long intervals, his wife urges him to seek compensation for their son, first from the killer Thorbjorn and later at the assembly. He receives humiliating responses, culminating when Thorbjorn hurls a cloth containing his son's teeth in his face. Despite his stiff limbs, Havard rises to perform an impressive deed as both a fighter and a skald. In a series of violent acts of revenge, Thorbjorn gathers a group of sixty armed and vindictive men. The hostilities are bloody but just, and Havard's claims are sustained in court. Toward the end of the saga, Havard is baptized in Norway and brings back timber to build a church in Iceland, where he is buried.

The saga survives only in young manuscripts, the oldest from the seventeenth century; the most important is AM 160 fol. (seventeenth century), although it has a small lacuna.

## The Saga of Hrafnkel Frey's Godi (*Hrafnkels saga Freysgoða*)

Dated to around 1300, it is a brief, cynical study of power and its means. The saga belongs to the end of the middle period. The saga writer seems to have no illusions about a just society in the Saga Age. Hrafnkel, the foremost chieftain in the area in the eastern part of Iceland, worships Frey; he has dedicated his horse Freyfaxi to the god and vowed to kill anyone who rides it. Einar, a young man from a poor family, hired as a shepherd by Hrafnkel, nevertheless rides Freyfaxi to gather missing sheep, prompting Hrafnkel to kill him. Reluctantly, he fulfills his duty due to his promise to the god. He offers Einar's father generous compensation, which the poor man declines. Instead, Einar's father persuades his nephew Sam to bring a case against Hrafnkel. With the help of two brothers from another region, they succeed in driving Hrafnkel from his farm Adalbol. They drown the horse, but spare Hrafnkel's life. Hrafnkel realizes that his worship of the gods is immoral, renounces Frey, and manages to flourish again in terms of power and wealth on another farm. When a servant woman mocks him six years later for being old and anxious, Hrafnkel kills Sam's brother, who has just returned from abroad and been uninvolved in the conflict. Hrafnkel then drives Sam off the farm from Adalbol, but spares Sam's life. At the end of the saga, Sam, who exceeded his rightful authority, is humiliated, while Hrafnkel retains or even increases his power.

90   *The Sagas of Icelanders*

The saga is preserved mainly in young manuscripts; there is only a small fragment in a vellum manuscript from ca. 1500 (AM 162 I fol.). Even though the text differs in the paper manuscripts, the differences are not significant enough to warrant distinct redactions. The various copies of the saga are divided into an A-version and a B-version. In the manuscripts, the latter constitutes the introduction to *The Saga of the People of Fljotsdal*.

### The Saga of Hord and the People of Holm
### (Harðar saga ok Hólmverja)

Dated to the fourteenth century, it belongs to the late medieval period. The saga is among the group with an outlaw as the protagonist—and in some respects it may even be considered an Icelandic Robin Hood tale. Hord is fostered by Geir's parents without love. As a young man, he spends fifteen years abroad with his foster brothers. In Sweden, he marries Helga, an earl's daughter. With the help of Odin, Hord breaks into a grave mound, where he obtains a cursed ring that brings about his death at the end of the saga. Back in Iceland, Hord gets involved in certain events because of his foster brothers, which result in their being outlawed. They barricade themselves on a steep small Island, Holm, in Hvalfjord. Here Hord, Helga, and the foster brothers stay with a band of criminals, the so-called "people of Holm." In the end, the entire region has turned against them. The neighboring farmers trick Hord and his men into believing that they will settle with them if they come ashore. The people of Holm accept the offer, despite Hord's suspicion and warnings, but when they reach shore, they are overpowered by the farmers and killed. On Holm, Helga realizes that something is wrong, and to save herself and Hord's sons, she swims several miles with each of the boys from the island. They are rescued by Hord's sister. After these events, several people try to get their hands on Hord's ring from the mound, but the ring disappears, when two women kill each other in an attempt to obtain it.

At the end of the saga, there is a reference to the priest Styrmir the Learned (1170–1245) as the informant about Hord, which has led several scholars to believe that Styrmir may have written an older version of the saga. A saga about Hord must have existed at least in the thirteenth century, as Sturla Þórðarson mentions a saga about Hord Grimkelsson in his redaction of the *Book of Settlements*.

The saga favors fantastic elements and shares a number of motifs with the sagas of ancient times: Hord breaks into the Viking Soti's burial mound to get his hands on a treasure, and Odin appears in the guise of the farmer Bjorn.

*The Saga of Hord and the People of Holm* is preserved in its entirety in one manuscript from the end of the fifteenth century (AM 556 a 4to); here the saga is called "Saga of the People of Holm" (*Hólmverja saga*). There also exists a small fragment from ca. 1390 to 1425 (AM 564 a 4to), where it is called "The Saga of Hord Grimkelsson" (*Harðar saga Grímkelssonar*).

## The Saga of Ref the Sly (*Króka-Refs saga*)

Dated to around 1325–1375, it belongs to the late medieval period. Related to European tales about Reynard the Fox, it is an entertaining and fast-paced narrative set in western Iceland and Greenland around 1000. Recent scholarship characterizes the saga as science fiction, due to the protagonist Ref's ("Fox") fantastic machinery—it is a saga written by a medieval author à la Jules Verne. Following his youth as a coal-biter, Ref becomes a hero by avenging his father. He is imaginative, talented, and resourceful, always finding solutions to problems. Although Ref's vengeance comes slowly, it is harsh. Despite having justice on his side, he must flee from place to place. He first leaves Breidafjord and then Iceland for Greenland, where he settles and where he kills a farmer and his four sons in one day. Later, he barricades himself in a fantastic fortification, which he has built. The construction has a sprinkling system and a wheeled boat, on which he can escape, if the fortification is conquered. Ref then travels to Norway, where he cunningly tricks the king with language inspired by skaldic kennings; before fleeing, he confesses to a killing in a way that no one can understand. After having deciphered the message, the king declares Ref an outlaw, but Ref is already far away. He visits the Danish King Svend and presents him with a polar bear and falcons. The king gives him land possessions and encourages him to maintain his recent pseudonym, Sigtrygg. He goes on a pilgrimage to Rome but dies en route as a devout Christian and is buried in a French monastery. One of his sons, who remained in Denmark, is said to be the ancestor of Archbishop Absalon.

The saga was written as entertaining fiction, drawing material from the *Book of Settlements*. Characters from *Gisli Sursson's Saga* and *The Saga of Havard of Isafjord* appear, as well as a motif from *The Tale of Audun from the West Fjords*, in which Audun also presents King Svend with a polar bear.

The saga is fully preserved in a single medieval manuscript from the second half of the fifteenth century (AM 471 4to), which also contains *The Saga of Thord Menace*, *The Saga of the People of Kjalarnes*, a romance, and three sagas of ancient times.

## The Saga of the Confederates (*Bandamanna saga*)

Believed to have been written around the middle of the thirteenth century, it belongs to the middle group of the sagas. This short saga, also known as "The Saga of Old Ofeig," takes place in the middle of the eleventh century in the northwestern part of Iceland, but the central scene is the Althing. The saga received its title from a group of greedy chieftains, who band together in a vulgar legal game. The protagonist is Ofeig, who is wise and knowledgeable about legal matters, but poor. Ofeig's son, Odd, who leaves home because of contempt for his father, achieves wealth and honor, whereupon he buys a large farm and becomes

92    *The Sagas of Icelanders*

a chieftain. When he has to go abroad again, he lets Ospak take care of the farm and the chieftaincy, but when he returns to the country, Ospak does not willingly return it. Subsequently, Ospak kills an innocent friend of Odd's, whereupon Odd takes legal action against him. Odd almost loses the case because of a trivial procedural mistake, even though it is clear to everyone that Odd is right in his case against Ospak. Odd's father Ofeig intervenes, using arguments and bribes to have the judges annul the judgment and declare Ospak an outlaw. The eight chieftains, who want to seize Odd's wealth, then attempt to have Odd sentenced for bribery, but again Ofeig wins over them in court. Odd marries a woman, a daughter of one of the chieftains who opposed him, and at the end of the saga, father and son are reconciled.

The saga paints a refined portrait of Ofeig: he is cynical and the arguments work in his favor. The saga's impalement of the corrupt magnates is a social satire at a high level.

The saga, extant in a long and a short, abridged, version, is preserved in its entirety in Möðruvallabók (AM 132 fol., ca. 1350). The manuscript contains the long redaction of the saga, which, according to the most recent editor of the saga, is the best. The short redaction is preserved in the manuscript GKS 2845 4to (ca. 1450).

### The Saga of the Greenlanders (Grænlendinga saga)

Dated to the beginning of the thirteenth century, though some propose ca. 1300, it is regarded as one of the oldest sagas of Icelanders. It deals with the Norse settlement of Greenland and expeditions to Vinland and shares content with *Eirik the Red's Saga*, which used it as a source. To some extent, the saga has roots in historical fact, for a viking dwelling by Norse Greenlanders from ca. 1000 was discovered by Helge Ingstad and Anne Stine Ingstad in L'Anse aux Meadows, Newfoundland, in 1960.

The saga begins when Eirik the Red and his father leave Norway because of some killings. After a brief stay in Iceland, Eirik the Red is outlawed due to more killings and he emigrates to Greenland. The saga recounts seven voyages to unknown lands. The young Bjarni sails off to Greenland, but he sails off course and past three unknown lands without going ashore. Eirik's son Leif is sent to Greenland with a priest by the Norwegian king to introduce Christianity, and he later names and explores the lands that Bjarni saw. Thorvald, another son of Eirik the Red, also sets sail but dies on the journey. Thorstein, the last of Eirik the Red's sons, takes off, but dies in the western Greenlandic settlement without reaching his destination. The fifth journey, led by Karlsefni, who is married to Gudrid, is an attempt to settle in the new world. In Vinland, the Norse trade with the natives, *skrælingjar*, and Gudrid gives birth to their son Snorri. The Norse Greenlanders and the *skrælingjar* come to blows, which makes them return to Greenland. The last journey ends in a disaster. The journey is undertaken at the initiative of Eirik the Red's daughter Freydis. She encourages two Norwegian brothers to join, but she breaks all the agreements between them and slaughters both brothers and their crew for no reason, even killing the women herself. After their return from Vinland, Karlsefni, Gudrid, and their son Snorri settle in Iceland. Shortly after Karlsefni's death, Gudrid goes on a pilgrimage and ends her days as a nun and an anchorite in Iceland. The saga concludes with an account of the lineage of several bishops descended from Snorri. Karlsefni is mentioned as an informant of the story.

The story, which is part of the larger narrative of Norway's missionary king, Olaf Tryggvason, has as its theme Christianity versus heathendom and serves to emphasize the king's zealous mission. Eirik the Red is depicted as a staunch pagan, who dismisses the priest brought by Leif the Lucky as a "swindler." Thorstein the Black in Greenland is also a heathen. When the people on his farm die, they appear as revenants. During Karlsefni and Gudrid's voyage to Vinland, a voice from above warns the Norsemen.

The saga is a reconstruction based on a number of *þættir* ("tales") found in various places in *The Great Saga of Olaf Tryggvason* in Flateyjarbók (GKS 1005 fol., ca. 1387–1395). Earlier editors have combined these tales to form a coherent saga text.

### The Saga of the People of Eyri (Eyrbyggja saga)

Believed to have been written around 1250, it belongs to the middle group of the sagas. It takes place primarily on Snæfellsnes in western Iceland and deals with the settlers of this area and their descendants. The plot stretches from the beginning of the ninth century until the beginning of the eleventh century. At the conclusion of the saga, it is called "The Saga of the People of Thorsnes, Eyri, and Alptafjord" ("Þórsnesinga ok Eyrbyggja ok Álptfirðinga saga"). The saga revolves around these three families, and also a fourth, the *Kjalleklingar* ("people from Kjallaksstadir"). The protagonist is the chieftain Snorri, head of the Thorsnes family, who is also known from *The Saga of the People of Laxardal*, which is referred to in this saga. At the beginning of the saga, Thorolf Mostrarskegg, ancestor of the Thorsnes family, emigrates to Iceland at the advice of "his dear friend Thor." He builds a large temple dedicated to Thor, and where an image of Thor drifts ashore, legal cases are settled. The place is so sacred that no one is allowed to relieve themselves there. The *Kjalleklingar*, however, do not want to go elsewhere for this purpose, so this sparks a conflict that exposes the Christian saga writer's disdain for paganism.

The saga tells of many supernatural events, revenants, and heathen practices, which, however, cannot be regarded as evidence of actual circumstances in heathen times. The household of the haunted farm Froda sees revenants gathering by the fire each evening, until the people on the farm carry out legal proceedings against the dead with the help of a priest, who pronounces verdicts and sentences

94    *The Sagas of Icelanders*

on the dead. Another revenant, who proves difficult to vanquish is Thorolf Lame-foot. When they dig him up to burn him, his corpse has not decomposed, and he resembles a troll.

The saga writer made use of a number of works in addition to *The Saga of the People of Laxardal*. A passage relating how Killer-Styr kills two Swedish berserks, one of whom has proposed to his daughter (he exhausts them before the killing by having them construct a path through a lava field, and then weakens them in a sauna), is taken almost verbatim from *The Saga of the Slayings on the Heath*. In addition, he used Styrmir's redaction of the *Book of Settlements* and *The Saga of Haakon the Good* (*Hákonar saga góða*).

*The Saga of the People of Eyri* is preserved incompletely in four medieval manuscripts (AM 162 E fol., ca. 1300; AM 309 4to, 1498; AM 445 b 4to, ca. 1390–1425; WolfAug 9 10 4to, ca. 1330–1370). The saga exists in an almost complete copy in a seventeenth-century copy of a medieval manuscript, Vatnshyrna (AM 448 4to), that was lost in the great fire of Copenhagen in 1728.

### The Saga of the People of Fljotsdal (*Fljótsdœla saga*)

It is set in eastern Iceland and is most often dated to the end of the Middle Ages, that is, between the end of the fifteenth century and 1550. Accordingly, it belongs to the youngest group. It was long regarded as the youngest of all sagas of Icelanders, but it has recently been argued that the saga may have been written toward the end of the fourteenth century.

The saga is written as a sequel to *The Saga of Hrafnkel Frey's Godi*, and focuses on the same characters and events as *The Saga of Droplaug's Sons*. The beginning of the saga relates a story about a troll, and thus provides Droplaug with a remarkable prehistory. Thorvald's journey, prompted by a disagreement with his brother, leads him to stay with an earl on Hjaltland, whose daughter Droplaug has been captured by a giant. The earl offers Droplaug's hand in marriage to whoever can rescue her, and Thorvald satisfies that role. He returns to Iceland with Droplaug, where she gives bith to their sons Grim and Helgi before Thorvald dies a short time later. The saga then recounts the same feud that *The Saga of Droplaug's Sons* revolves around: Grim and Helgi's bloody conflict with Helgi Asbjarnarson. The saga mentions that Droplaug is accused of having had relations with more than one man, but unlike *The Saga of Droplaug's Sons*, the incident is not tied to Helgi Asbjarnarson and thus leaves the cause of the conflict unclear. The saga writer weaves in a narrative about the unintentional killing of Thidrandi by the Norwegian Gunnar, which is followed by an extensive description of his pursuit. The story of Gunnar Thidrandabani ("killer of Þiðrandi") is also found in *The Saga of the People of Laxardal*, and in Gunnar's own *þáttr*: *The Tale of Gunnar, the Slayer of Thidrandi* (*Gunnars þáttr Þiðrandabana*). The conclusion of the saga is missing: it breaks off, when Grim and Helgi, as noble heathens, ravage a heathen temple.

The saga writer made use of a number of sagas: *The Saga of Hrafnkel Frey's Godi*, *The Saga of Droplaug's Sons*, *The Tale of Gunnar, the Slayer of Thidrandi*, *The Saga of the People of Laxardal*, *Njal's Saga*, *The Saga of Hallfred the Troublesome Poet*, and *The Saga of Thorstein the White*. It has been suggested that he perhaps knew Möðruvallabók (AM 132 fol., ca. 1350), in which many of these sagas are preserved.

The saga is preserved exclusively in young manuscripts; the most important is AM 551 c 4to from the first half of the seventeenth century.

### The Saga of the People of Floi (Flóamanna saga)

Dated between 1290 and 1330, it belongs to the late medieval period. The saga writer made use of sagas of Icelanders, sagas of ancient times, and hagiographic literature; in terms of genre the saga is a hybrid. The first nine chapters, dealing with the settlement, are based primarily on the *Book of Settlements* (Sturla Þórðarson's redaction). The saga then focuses on Thorgils *Qrrabeinsstjúpr* ("Scar-leg's stepson"), who, according to the saga, is an ancestor of bishop Saint Thorlak. Already as a young boy, Thorgils does not hesitate to kill a horse in order to participate in games with older boys, and at the age of nine, he is able to row a boat in a storm. As a young man, he travels to Norway, where he impresses King Harald Graafeld ("Grey-cloak"). While abroad, he kills a revenant and vikings; goes raiding; collects taxes for Earl Haakon in the Hebrides; and finally he finds a wife, whom he later hands over to his friend. In Iceland, he marries again—to Thorey. When Christianity is introduced in Iceland, Thorgils is among the first to convert. The heathen god Thor immediately begins to harass him, appearing in his dreams, accusing him of being a traitor, and killing his cattle. Thorgils is invited to Greenland by Eirik the Red. Two groups set off, a Christian and a heathen. After a rough journey at sea, where they are harassed by Thor, they are shipwrecked at a desolate spot in Greenland and cannot find any inhabited regions. Soon the members of the heathen group die of disease and hunger, and only a few men survive. When Thorgils and his men return to the hut after exploring the inland ice, they find Thorgils' wife murdered. To save the baby boy, Thorgils cuts his own breast to breastfeed him and places embers under his feet to stay awake while nursing the baby. After many adversities, the survivors find inhabited regions, only to realize, that Eirik the Red is a villain. They sail back toward Iceland, but in a storm at sea Thorgils' infant boy dies. In Iceland, Thorgils remarries, and though his young bride considers him old, their marriage thrives. Thorgils dies at an old age and lies buried by a church.

The saga is extant in a shorter and a longer redaction that is considered closer to the original. The longer redaction is preserved only in fragments; the oldest is AM 445 b 4to (ca. 1390–1425). The short redaction is preserved in its entirety in young paper manuscripts; the most important are AM 517 4to (ca. 1700) and AM 516 4to (seventeenth century).

96   *The Sagas of Icelanders*

### The Saga of the People of Kjalarnes (Kjalnesinga saga)

Dated to around 1310–1320, it belongs to the late medieval period. This short saga takes place primarily around 900 on Kjalarnes near modern Reykjavík, with much of its action occurring in Norway.

The saga tells of the chieftain Thorgrim, who builds a grand temple dedicated to Thor which requires human and animal sacrifices and temple-taxes from all locals. The protagonist Bui, who is regarded as strange because he refuses to sacrifice, burns down the temple. Bui is sentenced to outlawry, and, after a series of bloody events, his foster mother Esja helps get him to Norway. At the court of Harald Fair-hair, Harald, aware of the temple burning, sends Bui to retrieve a chessboard from the troll Dofri as punishment. Frid, Dofri's daughter, allows Bui into the mountain cave, where they sleep together. Bui manages to leave with the chessboard, and Frid tells him she is expecting his child, whom she will send to him, if it is a boy, when he is twelve years old. Upon his return to the king, Bui is asked to fight a *blámaðr*, before he receives permission to return to Iceland. Back home, the conflicts are settled, and Bui marries. At the end of the saga, Bui and Frid's son, Jokul, arrives to seek acknowledgment of their kinship. Bui refuses and proposes a wrestling match to decide the matter. Jokul mortally wounds Bui, who is buried in the church. Jokul leaves Iceland, and the saga comments that nothing more is heard of him. But *Jokul Buason's Tale*, which continues the story, reports that after this event, Jokul travels to Greenland.

The saga depicts conflicts between pagan Norsemen and Christians with Celtic roots and with a focus on heathen worship. Its descriptions of heathendom lack historical accuracy but offer insight into medieval Christian views of paganism. The saga is one of the sagas of Icelanders that contains the most supernatural elements.

The saga exists in four different versions. It survives in a single vellum manuscript from the late Middle Ages (AM 471 4to, ca. 1450–1550) and in various post-medieval paper manuscripts (AM 164 h fol., AM 504 4to, both from the seventeenth century, and AM 560 c 4to from 1700 to 1725).

### The Saga of the People of Laxardal (Laxdœla saga)

One of the longer sagas of Icelanders, it is believed to have been written between 1230 and 1260. It follows a family in western Iceland across generations. The saga unfolds as a triangular drama, which culminates in the deaths of the two cousins and foster brothers Kjartan and Bolli, who are both enamored of Gudrun. Betrayed love and feelings of rejection result in a chain of acts of revenge, which lead to the demise of both foster brothers. Inspired by courtly literature, the saga's tragic love story finds parallels in Icelandic heroic poetry. It shares characters with *Njal's Saga* and *Egil's Saga*; including Hallgerd's father Hoskuld, his half-brother Hrut, and Egil Skallagrimsson's daughter Thorgerd. The saga stands out for its focus on remarkable women and for having a female protagonist. In the introduction, Unn the Deep-minded settles in Iceland after years in Scotland, and establishes a magnificent farm. There is also Melkorka, a female slave from Ireland bought by Hoskuld at a market and kept as a concubine. She pretends to be unable to speak, but is found out, when she secretly converses one time with her son by Hoskuld. She is one of the very few slaves in the sagas of Icelanders who enjoys respect, but then it also turns out that she is the daughter of the king of Ireland. Thorgerd, Egil Skallagrimsson's daughter, also plays a prominent role in the saga. It is through her influence that Bolli's vengeance is carried out, who was raised in her home. Smaller, but still influential, roles are played by Thurid, who exchanges her daughter for a sword; and Aud, unique among saga women, who dons trousers, arms herself, and singlehandedly seeks revenge. The real protagonist is Gudrun Osvifsdottir, whom we follow through her four marriages; her unresolved relationship with Kjartan; and finally, her life as an anchorite, a Christian, and a penitent.

The saga is transmitted in numerous manuscripts, with a complete version found in Möðruvallabók (AM 132 fol., ca. 1350). In this manuscript, the saga is followed by *Bolli Bollason's Tale* about one of Gudrun and Bolli's sons.

### The Saga of the People of Ljosavatn (Ljósvetninga saga)

Dated to around 1230–1250, it belongs to the oldest group of sagas. Set in the mid-eleventh century around Eyjafjord in northern Iceland, it revolves around the conflict between two powerful families from Möðruvellir and Ljosavatn. The saga may be divided into two parts. It is introduced by an account of the friendship of Gudmund the Powerful and Thorgeir from Ljosavatn, who is also known for his role in the decision about the conversion to Christianity, as detailed in *Njal's Saga*. A bloody conflict arises between Gudmund and Thorgeir's sons, which results in Gudmund's killing one of the sons. The conflict with Thorgeir's sons continues in the second part of the saga, where one of Gudmund's sons is killed. The saga also tells of the antagonistic relationship between Gudmund the Powerful and his brother Einar. The saga is atypical of the sagas of Icelanders, in which the plot is normally chronologically continuous. It jumps back in time and recounts an episode from the brothers' youth: Gudmund's bald foster father was sleeping outside one day when a midge landed on his head. Gudmund wanted to whisk it away with his hand, but Einar instead encouraged him to use an axe nicking the foster father's head, who woke up thinking that Gudmund wanted to attack him. Gudmund then realized he could not trust his brother.

The saga's transmission is problematic. It exists in two redactions, both believed to be revisions of the same thirteenth-century original. The A-redaction, considered to be the older, is preserved in the fragmentary AM 561 4to (ca. 1400) and contains only the saga's beginning. Only the longer C-redaction preserves the complete saga, but it exists only in young manuscripts. This redaction, of

98   *The Sagas of Icelanders*

which a fifteenth-century fragment survives (AM 162 C 1 fol.), is believed to have been written in the fourteenth century. The C-redaction has incorporated three *þættir* ("tales"): *The Tale of Sorli* (*Sǫrla þáttr*), about the love between Sorli and Gudmund's daughter Thordis, initially opposed by Gudmund; *The Tale of Ofeig* (*Ófeigs þáttr*), which describes Gudmund's conflicts with his brother Einar; and *The Tale of Vodu-Brand* (*Vǫðu-Brands þáttr*) about Brand's tyrannical behavior.

### The Saga of the People of Reykjadal and of Killer-Skuta (Reykdœla saga ok Víga-Skútu)

Sometimes entitled *Vémundar saga og Víga-Skútu* ("The Saga of Vemund and Killer-Skuta"), which has generally been dated to around 1250, it belongs to the oldest period of the sagas of Icelanders. Set in northern Iceland between Eyjafjord and Thingeyrar, its narrative style is marked by an uneven structure and repetitive phrases, almost formulaic, which many scholars consider the result of an oral tradition. Accordingly, some scholars have dated it to the very oldest period, around 1210–1220, as an early attempt to write a saga of Icelanders. Phrases like "one says," "it is said," or "it is told" are used around one hundred times. The saga also employs direct speech and dialogue to a lesser degree than the other sagas of Icelanders. Additionally, the writer discusses the accuracy of his information and presents alternative versions.

The narrative deviates from the common narrative of a young man traveling abroad to gain wealth and honor and focuses instead on feuds and vengeance for slain kinsmen. The saga can be divided into two parts: the first revolves around Vemund and the wise and peace-seeking chieftain Askel from Reykjadal, who is depicted as a noble heathen. Askel conceals a mortal blow from a battle, because he is aware of his family's inclination for conflict. Askel's son, Killer-Skuta, avenges his father in the second part of the saga, which revolves around his conflicts with his father-in-law Killer-Glum. Chapter 26 in this saga is almost identical to Chapter 16 in *Killer-Glum's saga*. It is uncertain whether *Killer-Glum's saga* drew from *The Saga of the People of Reykjadal and of Killer-Skuta*, or vice versa, though many scholars lean toward the former.

The saga is extant in a vellum manuscript from ca. 1400 (AM 561 4to), which starts only with Chapter 13 to the end with two lacunae. Around thirty younger copies all derive from this manuscript, including the missing text.

### The Saga of the People of Svarfadardal (Svarfdœla saga)

Dated to 1350–1400, it belongs to the late medieval period. However, in the thirteenth century, an account of the people in this valley in northwestern Iceland evidently existed, since the *Book of Settlements* tells of the early inhabitants of Svarfadardal. The older version is generally believed to form the basis of

The Sagas of Icelanders. A Survey  99

the surviving saga. A large part of the saga is lost, however, and the preserved sections appear to derive from two different sagas in terms of content and expression. The first nine chapters are reminiscent of a saga of ancient times and take place in northern Norway. They recount the adventures of the coal-biter Thorstein, who rouses himself after having long lain around by the fire. After a series of fights against Vikings, he arrives at the court of the Swedish earl, harassed by a berserk who wants to marry the earl's daughter. Thorstein defeats the berserk and obtains the girl's hand in marriage. Here, there is a lacuna in the saga (beginning in Chapter 9); when the saga continues, the setting and the style are different. In the second part of the saga, another Thorstein, possibly a descendant, settles in northern Iceland and becomes a chieftain in Svarfadardal. The saga recounts conflicts among the inhabitants of the valley and features Klaufi. On the sly, he marries Yngvild Fair-cheek, who manages to have him killed. But even after his death, he returns as a haunting revenant, carrying his severed head, reciting verses, while knocking on doors with his head. After Klaufi's demise, Yngvild is reluctantly married to Skidi, a disfigured slave, for his aid in battle, but on the condition that if his cleft lip does not heal within five years, she retains the right to divorce him. When a settlement has almost been reached by the feuding parties, Yngvild disrupts it by referring to Skidi's lip, which has not closed. During a controversy, Skidi kills Karl, which prompts Karl's son to exact brutal vengeance against Yngvild later on. She is sold as a slave and deeply humiliated, making this one of the most misogynistic episodes in the sagas of Icelanders. Eventually, she recognizes her mistakes, though by then she is shunned by everyone, and she ends up committing suicide. This conclusion seems to echo similar passages in romances.

The saga is not preserved in its entirety. Only a single vellum leaf survives from the Middle Ages (AM 445 c II 4to, ca. 1450). Copies exist in paper manuscripts, deriving from a copy of a preserved manuscript from the mid-seventeenth century (AM 161 fol.). No manuscript contains the complete text.

### The Saga of the People of Vatnsdal (Vatnsdœla saga)

Likely written between 1270 and 1280, that is, in the middle period, it is set in Vatnsdal, northern Iceland. It follows five generations of descendants of Ketil the Strong from Romsdal, Norway. The saga spans the period from the ninth century to around 1000. The first part of the saga takes place in Norway, where it follows Thorstein, who does away with a feared robber. Atypical for the sagas, the narrator provides insights into Thorstein's thoughts before his fight with the robber, who turns out to be the son of an earl in Götaland. Acknowledging Thorstein's luck, the dying robber urges him to seek out his family and marry his sister. Thorstein marries the sister and becomes close friends with the earl. Their firstborn son is named Ingimund after the earl. When Ingimund comes of age, he fights on the side of Harald Fair-hair, and even though his foster brother goes to

100   *The Sagas of Icelanders*

Iceland to avoid having to submit to royal power, Ingimund chooses to remain in Norway; as he says, he does not want to go to "that desolate outcrop." Soon after, a Sámi woman predicts his journey to Iceland, but he repeats that he will not go to that "wilderness." The woman tells him that an amulet of Frey, which he had received from the king, awaits him in Iceland at his destined settlement. Ingimund resigns, and with the king's permission he sails to Iceland, and when he reaches Vatnsdal, he finds his amulet. He settles in Vatnsdal and becomes a respected and just chieftain. His five sons, each with a different temperament, fight to maintain order in the valley, which is terrorized by a witch and her son Hrolleif, who eventually kill the peace-loving Ingimund. After Ingimund's death, his son Thorstein, a noble heathen, takes over the chieftaincy. After the sons have slain Hrolleif, villains and magicians once again trouble the valley. A conflict arises between Ingimund's sons and Berg and Finnbogi the Mighty, the protagonist of *The Saga of Finnbogi the Mighty*. Toward the end of the saga, Bishop Fridrek and the missionary Thorvald arrive in Iceland in order to preach Christianity, known from *The Tale of Thorvald the Far-Travelled*. Thorkel Scratcher, the last person of the family chronicled in the saga, is one of the very few people in the region who welcomes the missionaries, and all the people in Vatnsdal are baptized.

Only a small fragment of the saga is preserved in a medieval manuscript (AM 445 b 4to, ca. 1390–1425), but there are paper manuscripts of the saga, which are reliable copies of a fourteenth-century manuscript.

### The Saga of the People of Vopnafjord (Vápnfirðinga saga)

Dated to around 1225–1250, it belongs to the oldest group of sagas. Set in northeastern Iceland, in the area around Vopnafjord, this short text features characters also found in other sagas: in *The Saga of Droplaug's Sons*, *The Saga of Thorstein the White*, and *Íslendingadrápa* ("Poem about Icelanders"). The main plot is a feud between the chieftains, Brodd-Helgi and Geitir, who at the beginning of the saga are close friends but eager to accumulate wealth. The conflict begins, when they kill a Norwegian to obtain his wealth—he was known for wearing a gold bracelet and sitting on a chest, rumoured to be full of gold and silver. But the law prevents them from taking over the Norwegian's possessions, which leaves them suspicious of each other, as each believes the other has stolen the Norwegian's bracelet and chest. Their greed and mistrust destroy their friendship and brings misery upon their closest relatives. Brodd-Helgi is married to Geitir's sister, Halla, who falls ill, whereafter he is betrothed to another woman, Thorgerd Silver, and he sends Halla away in a humiliating manner, while keeping her money. The conflict culminates, when the pacifist Geitir kills Brodd-Helgi. After this, the saga focuses mainly on Geitir and Brodd-Helgi's sons. At Thorgerd Silver's instigation, Bjarni, Brodd-Helgi's son, who was raised by Geitir, reluctantly slays his foster father. He repents and sits holding the dying man

*The Sagas of Icelanders. A Survey*    101

in his arms, a scene reminiscent of Bolli's killing of Kjartan in *The Saga of the People of Laxardal*. In an ensuing fight between Bjarni and Geitir's son, Thorkel, Thorkel is severely injured, but subsequently Bjarni sends a doctor to heal him. Bjarni has a leading role in resolving the conflict: Bjarni invites Thorkel, who is ill, poor, and unable to take care of his farm—to move in with him, promising to take care of him and his household. The saga concludes by mentioning that Iceland's saint, Thorlak (d. 1193), is descended from Thorkel.

The saga is poorly preserved, which negatively affects its plot. Aside from a vellum manuscript from ca. 1420 to 1450 (AM 162 C fol.), it survives only in young paper manuscripts. In the seventeenth century, a more complete vellum manuscript existed, but copies reveal that this manuscript was already in poor condition, when it was copied: all copies have a lacuna of about two pages in the exemplar, and several passages are transmitted defectively.

### The Saga of the Slayings on the Heath (*Heiðarvíga saga*)

It is considered one of the oldest sagas of Icelanders due to its unrefined language, style, and influence on later sagas. Generally, it has been dated to around 1200, though some scholars suggest a later date, noting possible borrowings from the younger *The Saga of the People of Laxardal*. The saga is set in mid-western Iceland.

The saga tells of a major battle between men from Hunavatn and Borgarfjord, occurring on the heath Tvidaegra ("Two Days' Journey") in western Iceland in 1014. The plot is split into two loosely connected parts. The first part focuses on Killer-Styr, who kills thirty-three men without paying compensation and defeats two berserks, one of whom has proposed to his daughter. Before killing them, Killer-Styr exhausts the berserks by making them construct a path through a lava field and he then weakens them in a sauna. This passage is also found almost verbatim in *The Saga of the People of Eyri*, which mentions *The Saga of the Slayings on the Heath* as its source. Killer-Styr is slain by the son of his last victim. Styr's son-in-law, the chieftain Snorri, also known from *The Saga of the People of Laxardal* and *The Saga of the People of Eyri*, then starts a vendetta. The saga's second part follows Bardi's quest for compensation for his brother's unjust killing. When legal avenues fail, he resorts to arms. People in Borgarfjord know of his plans and regularly ask mockingly "that wouldn't be Bardi now, would it?" Eventually, they learn that Bardi is indeed coming, which leads to the second part of the saga and culminates in the great battle at Tvidaegra. In the ensuing judicial settlement, reconciliation occurs when an old man, having lost both of his sons in the battle, movingly advocates for a settlement and sets aside his own interests. Afterward, Bardi travels to Norway, where Saint Olaf refuses to receive him, because he is a heathen. He ends his days fighting with the Varangians in Constantinople.

The transmission of the saga is unusual and problematic, which leaves its mark on it. The first fifteen chapters were destroyed in the Copenhagen fire of

## 102 *The Sagas of Icelanders*

1728 and survive only in an eighteenth-century reconstruction by Jón Ólafsson from Grunnavík. Jón Ólafsson, who worked as scribe for the manuscript collector Árni Magnússon, mentioned in his introduction to the reconstruction that he copied the saga once around the turn of the year 1727–1728 from a parchment manuscript which Árni Magnússon had borrowed from Sweden. This copy was also lost in the fire, and Jón Ólafsson reconstructed the saga from memory and a list of words and expressions in the saga that he had made. Thus, in the first fifteen chapters of the saga, there are two layers: the reconstructed saga text itself and Jón Ólafsson's comments on the reconstruction ("as far as I remember" or "as is written in the saga," which he writes, when he uses a citation from his list of words).

The rest of the text is preserved in the medieval fragment from ca. 1300 (Holm perg 18 4to and Lbs frg 1). Jón Ólafsson's copy is found in AM 450 b 4to (1730).

### The Saga of the Sworn Brothers (*Fóstbrœðra saga*)

It is set in the Westfjords of Iceland, Greenland, and Norway. Scholars do not agree on whether the saga should be dated to ca. 1200, which would make it one of the oldest sagas, or to ca. 1300, which would place it at the end of the middle period. The saga deals with Thorgeir and the skald Thormod. They become sworn brothers, adhering to an honor code of brutality, silence, and vengeance. They commit one killing after another, until Thorgeir becomes so uncontrollable that he wants to measure himself against Thormod, and for this reason they part ways. Thorgeir is outlawed and leaves Iceland, but in the retinue of King Olaf the Saint in Norway, he manages to control his violent temper. Thormod and Thorgeir are sworn brothers and this requires that they avenge each other's death. When Thorgeir is killed, Thormod sets out on a lengthy vendetta. He ends his days serving King Olaf the Saint and dies alongside him in the battle of Stiklestad (1030). Being a typical saga skald, Thormod is drawn to women, and his love affairs are rash and messy. He receives his byname *Kolbrúnarskáld* ("Kolbrun's poet") due to an affair, whereas the manly Thorgeir is indifferent to love. Thorgeir's renowned courage leads people to remove his heart after his death in order to discern what constitutes such a courageous heart. (As it turns out, the heart is notably smaller compared to the large, blood-filled hearts of cowardly men.)

The saga has been transmitted in three redactions: Flateyjarbók (GKS 1005 fol., ca. 1387–1395), Hauksbók (AM 544 4to, ca. 1300), and Möðruvallabók (AM 132 fol., ca. 1350). The oldest manuscript is Hauksbók, which lacks the beginning of the saga and is somewhat abridged compared to the two other redactions. In Möðruvallabók, several leaves of the saga are missing. The Flateyjarbók redaction of the saga contains learned and theological digressions. In this manuscript, the saga forms part of a larger narrative about Saint Olaf. Flateyjarbók

The Sagas of Icelanders. A Survey    103

is the only manuscript containing a preface by the redactor, explaining how the saga might be understood in the fourteenth century.

### The Saga of Thord Menace (Þórðar saga hreðu)

Belonging to the late medieval period, it is believed to have been written around 1350. It is set in northwestern Iceland, east of the Westfjords. The saga writer knew several sagas of ancient times, at least *The Saga of Hrolf Kraki* (*Hrólfs saga kraka*), *The Saga of Hervor and Heidrek* (*Hervarar saga ok Heiðreks*), and *The Saga of Ragnar Lothbrok* [Hairy-breeches] (*Ragnars saga loðbrókar*), along with the *Book of Settlements* and *Njal's Saga*. Thord is the protagonist throughout the saga. He kills King Harald's brother and flees from Norway to Iceland. A strong and skilled artisan, Thord lands in Midfjord, where he falls out with the chieftain Skeggi. Thord refuses to submit to Skeggi's rule over the region, and when Thord kills one of Skeggi's family members, the hostilities escalate. Earlier, Thord had rescued Skeggi's son Eid from a capsized boat. Eid stays with Thord as his foster son, despite Skeggi's disapproval. Eid often mediates between Skeggi and Thord and sides with Thord during an armed encounter. Because of his enormous strength, Thord repeatedly wards off attempts to kill him and becomes renowned throughout the land. In between the battles, which occasionally have comic interludes, Thord finds time to build solid houses or work on his ships. According to the saga, one of Thord's houses was still standing during Bishop Egil Eyjolfsson's time (1332–1341). Ultimately, Eid reconciles the conflicting parties. The saga has a happy ending with a comment from the saga writer that he has not heard any more authentic accounts about Thord.

The saga exists in two versions. One is fragmentary in that it contains only parts of the introduction and the conclusion (AM 564 a 4to, ca. 1390–1425). This version draws on kings' sagas and *The Saga of the People of Laxardal*. The other version, which has been preserved in its entirety in paper manuscripts, deals with the protracted feud between Thord and Skeggi from Midfjord. The most important manuscript of this version is from the first half of the fifteenth century (AM 551 d β 4to), though it is only a fragment, and most of the saga's text is found in seventeenth-century copies.

### The Saga of Thorstein the White (Þorsteins saga hvíta)

Extraordinarily short Saga of Icelanders, it has generally been dated to ca. 1275–1300. Accordingly, it belongs to the middle group. There are several overlaps between this saga and parts of *The Saga of the People of Vopnafjord*, for which the saga was likely written as an introduction. Set in northeastern Iceland around 900, the saga shares motifs with *The Saga of Gunnlaug Serpent-Tongue*, *The Saga of the People of Laxardal*, and *The Saga of Bjorn, Champion of the Hitardal People*. Thorstein the Fair, a young and promising man, gives another

104    *The Sagas of Icelanders*

man, Einar, a half-share of his ship and enters a financial partnership with him, attempting in each and every way to advance him. But Thorstein the Fair remains more respected, wherever they go. Thorstein the Fair is betrothed to Helga, a beautiful woman, who promises to wait for him, while he again travels to Norway. During the voyage, Thorstein the Fair falls ill with scurvy. Einar and the other travel companions mock him and leave him all winter in a storehouse. Einar and Thorstein the Fair divide their property, and Einar returns to Iceland, claiming that Thorstein suffered a gruesome death, and marries Helga. When Thorstein the Fair returns to Iceland, he visits Einar, who refuses to give him compensation, and so Thorstein the Fair kills him. Einar's father seeks revenge, kills Thorstein's brothers and has Thorstein outlawed. Thorstein leaves for five years, then returns and surrenders to Thorstein the White, who invites him to move to his farm. Thorstein the Fair marries Helga and is treated like a son by Thorstein the White. When Brodd-Helgi comes of age, Thorstein the White advises Thorstein the Fair to leave the country. The saga concludes with brief references to the friendship and animosity between Brodd-Helgi and Geitir as is related in *The Saga of the People of Vopnafjord*.

The title of the saga is somewhat misleading, for even though Thorstein the White appears both at the beginning and at the end of the saga, the protagonist is really Thorstein the Fair. Nonetheless, Thorstein the White is important, considering his reconciliary gesture at the end of the saga.

The saga survives only in two seventeenth-century paper manuscripts (AM 156 fol. and AM 496 4to).

### Thorstein Sidu-Hallsson's Saga (*Þorsteins saga Síðu-Hallssonar*)

Likely written around the mid-thirteenth century, it belongs to the middle period. It is set primarily in eastern Iceland in the eleventh century. It follows Thorstein Sidu-Hallsson, who is also known from kings' sagas. It relates that Thorstein transfers his chieftaincy to Thorhadd before traveling to the Orkney Islands and Ireland, where he participates in the Battle of Clontarf in 1014. He then goes to Norway. Back in Iceland after three years abroad with kings and earls, Thorstein finds that Thorhadd refuses to give up the chieftaincy, until Thorstein threatens to attack him. Thorstein orders Thorhadd to leave the farm, on which he is staying, but Thorhadd again refuses, and as a result Thorstein burns down the farm, though without killing anyone. As a result, animosity flares up, and Thorhadd spreads slander about Thorstein (that he is a woman every ninth night and sleeps with men). Thorstein ignores the mockery until his deceased mother appears to him in a dream and incites him to seek revenge. Dreams play a large role in this saga. In addition to Thorstein's dream, there are fourteen prophetic dreams, and in a single chapter no fewer than twelve dreams are interpreted for Thorhadd. The day after the dream, Thorstein kills Thorhadd's sons. At this point, there is a lacuna, but a preserved poem, *Poem about Icelanders*, indicates that Thorstein

The Sagas of Icelanders. A Survey    105

subsequently also kills Thorhadd. The saga concludes with a genealogy, which gives an account of Sidu-Hall's descendants, including Saint Jón, bishop of Hólar.

The saga contains a reference to *Njal's Saga*, which is considered younger than *Thorstein Sidu-Hallsson's Saga*. It is believed that this reference was added by a scribe at a later time.

The saga is not preserved in its entirety. The first chapters and some leaves toward the end are lacking. It is transmitted in young paper manuscripts, of which the most important are JS 435 4to (ca. 1700–1900) and AM 142 fol. (1690–1697). Neither manuscript contains a complete version of the saga. AM 142 fol. is the longer of the two but lacks both the beginning and the end.

### Valla-Ljot's Saga (*Valla-Ljóts saga*)

It is a short saga set primarily in Svarfadardal, northern Iceland. It has been dated to between 1220 and 1240 and thus belongs to the oldest group of sagas. Initially, the saga follows three brothers, Halli, Hrolf, and Bodvar, whose father dies. Subsequently, a freed slave, Torfi, seeks to marry their mother. Despite Halli's objections, his mother and brothers accept the marriage proposal. After a humiliating quarrel, in which Torfi insults Halli, Halli kills Torfi. Halli becomes friends with Gudmund the Powerful, but eventually he becomes dissatisfied with being his inferior, he therefore moves—despite warnings—to Svarfadardal, where Valla-Ljot is a chieftain. Halli arrogantly accuses Ljot of working on St. Michael's day and boasts about it. Ljot retaliates by killing him; the matter is settled, but Halli's brother Hrolf nonetheless kills a nephew of Ljot. The acts of vengeance escalate and culminate in a direct confrontation between Valla-Ljot and Gudmund the Powerful. The saga concludes with a settlement between Ljot and Gudmund, which satisfies both parties.

Valla-Ljot is descended from the people in Svarfadardal, the subject of *The Saga of the People of Svarfadardal*, where it is noted that "there are many stories of Valla-Ljot" (Chapter 29). Gudmund the Powerful is also known from other sagas, notably *The Saga of the People of Ljosavatn*, in which he is portrayed with less sympathy than in *Valla-Ljot's Saga*.

The saga survives only in young manuscripts; the most important are AM 161 fol. and AM 496 4to, both from the seventeenth century.

### Viglund's Saga (*Víglundar saga*)

Belonging to the late medieval period, it is believed to have been written around 1400. It is also known under the title "The saga of Thorgrim the Elegant and Viglund the Fair" (*Þorgríms saga prúða ok Víglundar væna*). Set during the reign of Harald Fair-hair, it takes place primarily on Snæfellsnes, western Iceland. It is a courtly love story about Viglund and Ketilrid, whose love is thwarted

106 *The Sagas of Icelanders*

because of enmity between their families. Nonetheless, they reveal courtliness and high morals. The saga is reminiscent of romances and especially the saga of ancient times *The Saga of Frithiof the Bold*, but it also contains motifs from the sagas of Icelanders. The saga makes reference to Bard *Snæfellsáss* ("God of Snæfell"). Like most of the saga heroes in love, Viglund recites a number of verses.

The theme is struck at the beginning of the saga, when the young lovers, Thorgrim and Olof, flee from Norway to Iceland to marry. Their son is Viglund, and Ketilrid, the neighbor's daughter, is fostered in their home. Viglund and Ketilrid fall in love, but the two sets of brothers are in conflict with one another. Viglund kills one of Ketilrid's brothers in self-defense and is forced to leave the country. While Viglund is in Norway, the two families are reconciled, and the fathers devise a plan. When Viglund returns, Ketilrid has been married to an old man, but it turns out to be a test for the two lovers and gives them a chance to show their great virtue. The saga concludes with several marriages, that of Viglund and Ketilrid, and two others.

Viglund, a skald, differs from the typical skald in the sagas of Icelanders. He is faithful, virtuous, level-headed, and ultimately marries his beloved.

The saga is preserved in two late medieval manuscripts, AM 551 a 4to (ca. 1500) and AM 510 4to (ca. 1550), and in a number of paper manuscripts.

# Literature

## Original Language Editions

Editions of the sagas of Icelanders can be found in:

*Brennu-Njáls saga*, ed. Sveinn Yngvi Egilsson. 2nd ed. (Reykjavík: Bjartur, 2003).

*Brennu-Njáls saga*. 3 vols. Ed. Guðbrandur Vigfússon and C. R. Unger (Kristiania [Oslo]: Malling, 1860–1868).

*Handskrifterna til Erik den Rödes saga*. Ed. Sven F. B. Jansson (Stockholm: Wahlström & Widstrand, 1945).

*Íslendingasögur*. 3 vols. Ed. Bragi Halldórsson, Jón Torfason, Sverrir Tómasson, and Örnólfur Thorsson (Reykjavík: Svart á hvítu, 1987).

Íslenzk fornrit. Vol. 2–14. Various editors. (Reykjavík: Hið íslenzka fornritafélag, 1933–1993).

## Manuscripts

The manuscripts mentioned in this book are listed below. The dating of the medieval manuscripts is based on the *Dictionary of Old Norse Prose* (onp.ku.dk). The list is structured according to (1) the place in which the manuscript is currently housed, (2) the size of the manuscript (folio/quarto). Between 1971 and 1997, the majority of the manuscripts containing sagas of Icelanders were transferred from Denmark to Iceland, where they are now housed. Approximately half of Árni Magnússon's collection of manuscripts is still preserved in Denmark, including the manuscripts of the king's sagas.

*Copenhagen*
*The Arnamagnæan Collection, Department of Nordic and Linguistic Studies, University of Copenhagen*

Folios
AM 226 fol. (ca. 1350–1360)

Quartos

AM 309 4to (1498)

108   *Literature*

AM 453 4to (seventeenth century)
AM 468 4to (ca. 1300–1325) Reykjabók
AM 544 4to (ca. 1300) (Hauksbók)
Hauksbók, see AM 544 4to
Reykjabók, see AM 468 4to

*Reykjavík*
*The Árni Magnússon Institute for Icelandic Studies, University of Iceland*

Folios

AM 132 fol. (ca. 1330–1370) (Möðruvallabók)
AM 133 fol. (ca. 1350) (Kálfalækjarbók)
AM 142 fol. (1690–1697)
AM 156 fol. (ca. 1650)
AM 158 fol. (ca. 1630–1675)
AM 160 fol. (seventeenth century)
AM 161 fol. (seventeenth century)
AM 162 A Φ fol. (ca. 1250)
AM 162 C fol. (ca. 1420–1450)
AM 162 C 1 fol. (ca. 1420–1450)
AM 162 E fol. (ca. 1300)
AM 162 F fol. (ca. 1350–1400)
AM 162 G fol. (ca. 1400–1500)
AM 162 I fol. (ca. 1500)
AM 164 h fol. (seventeenth century)
GKS 1005 fol. (ca. 1387–1395) (Flateyjarbók)
Flateyjarbók, see GKS 1005 fol.
Kálfalækjarbók, see AM 133 fol.
Möðruvallabók, see AM 132 fol.

Quartos

AM 443 4to (seventeenth century)
AM 445 b 4to (ca. 1390–1425 (Pseudo-Vatnshyrna)
AM 445 c I 4to (ca. 1390–1425) (Pseudo-Vatnshyrna)
AM 445 c II 4to (ca. 1450)
AM 448 4to (ca. 1700)
AM 450 b 4to (1730)
AM 453 4to (seventeenth century)
AM 463 4to (1663)
AM 471 4to (ca. 1450–1500)
AM 486 4to (seventeenth century)
AM 496 4to (ca. 1640)
AM 504 4to (seventeenth century)
AM 510 4to (ca. 1550)
AM 516 4to (seventeenth century)

*Literature* 109

AM 517 4to (ca. 1700)
AM 551 a 4to (ca. 1500)
AM 551 c 4to (ca. 1630–1640)
AM 551 d β 4to (ca. 1400–1450)
AM 554 i 4to (seventeenth century)
AM 556 a 4to (ca. 1475–1500)
AM 557 4to (ca. 1420–1450) (Skálholtsbók)
AM 560 c 4to (1700–1725)
AM 561 4to (ca. 1400)
AM 564 a 4to (ca. 1390–1425) (Pseudo-Vatnshyrna)
GKS 2845 4to (ca. 1450)
GKS 2870 4to (ca. 1300) (Gráskinna)
Gráskinna, see GKS 2870 4to
Skálholtsbók, see AM 557 4to

*National and University Library of Iceland*

JS 435 4to (1687–1877?)

Lbs frg 1 (1300–1350)

*Stockholm*
*Royal Library*

Holm perg 18 4to (ca. 1300–1350)

*Wolfenbüttel*
*Herzog August Bibliothek*

WolfAug 9 10 4to (ca. 1330–1370)

## English Translations

The most recent translation of all of the sagas of Icelanders is:
*The Complete Sagas of Icelanders Including 49 Tales,* 5 vols. Ed. Viðar Hreinsson. Reykja-
   vík: Leifur Eiríksson Publishing, 1997. Unless otherwise mentioned, the citations
   from the sagas of Icelanders above are from this edition. Some of these translations
   were reprinted in *The Sagas of Icelanders: A Selection.* New York: Penguin, 1997.
In addition, there are translations of individual sagas. A select list appears below.
*The Confederates and Hen-Thorir.* 1975. Trans. Hermann Pálsson. Edinburgh: Southside.
*Egil's Saga.* 1975. Trans. Christine Fell and John Lucas. Toronto: University of Toronto
   Press.
*Egil's Saga.* 1960. Trans. Gwyn Jones. Syracuse, NY: Syracuse University Press.
*Eirik the Red and other Icelandic Sagas.* 1961. Trans. Gwyn Jones. Oxford: Oxford Uni-
   versity Press.
*Eyrbyggja Saga.* 1959. Trans. Paul Schach and Lee M. Hollander. Lincoln: University of
   Nebraska Press.

110   *Literature*

*Eyrbyggja Saga.* 1973. Trans. Hermann Pálsson and Paul Edwards. Toronto: University of Toronto Press.

*Four Icelandic Sagas.* 1935. Trans. Gwyn Jones. Oxford: Oxford University Press.

*Grettir's Saga.* 1974. Trans. Denton Fox and Hermann Pálsson. Toronto: University of Toronto Press.

*Hrafnkel's Saga and Other Icelandic Stories.* 1971. Trans. Hermann Pálsson. Harmondsworth: Penguin.

*Laxdæla Saga.* 1969. Trans. Magnus Magnusson and Hermann Pálsson. Harmondsworth: Penguin.

*Njal's Saga.* 1960. Trans Hermann Pálsson and Magnus Magnusson. Harmondsworth: Penguin.

*The Saga of Gisli.* 1963. Trans. George Johnston. London: Dent.

*The Saga of Gisli: Son of Sour.* 1936. Trans. Ralph B. Allen. New York: Harcourt-Brace.

*The Saga of Gunnlaug Serpent-Tongue.* 1957. Ed. and trans. Randolph Quirk and Peter Foote. London: Viking Society for Northern Research.

*The Sagas of the Kormak and The Sworn Brothers.* 1949. Trans. Lee M. Hollander. Princeton, NJ: Princeton University Press.

*Vinland Sagas: The Norse Discovery of America.* 1965. Trans. Magnus Magnusson and Hermann Pálsson. Harmondsworth: Penguin.

## Secondary Literature and Further Reading

***Icelandic names are listed under their first name.***

Andersson, Theodore M. 1967. *The Icelandic Family Saga: An Analytic Reading.* Cambridge, MA: Harvard University Press.

Andersson, Theodore M. 2006. *The Growth of the Medieval Icelandic Sagas (1180–1280).* Ithaca, NY and London: Cornell University Press.

Ármann Jakobsson. 2013. *Nine Saga Studies: The Critical Interpretation of the Icelandic Sagas.* Reykjavík: University of Iceland Press.

Ármann Jakobsson and Sverrir Jakobsson, eds. 2017. *The Routledge Research Companion to the Medieval Icelandic Sagas.* Oxford: Routledge.

Arnold, Martin. 2003. *The Post-Classical Icelandic Family Saga.* Scandinavian Studies 9. Lewiston, ME, Queenston, and Lampeter: The Edwin Mellen Press.

Bampi, Massimiliano, Carolyne Larrington and Sif Rikhardsdottir, eds. *A Critical Companion to Old Norse Literary Genre.* Cambridge: Cambridge University Press.

Bredsdorff, Thomas. 2001. *Chaos and Love: The Philosophy of the Icelandic Family Sagas.* Trans. John Tucker. Copenhagen: Museum Tusculanum Press.

Byock, Jesse L. 1982. *Feud in the Icelandic Saga.* Berkeley: University of California Press.

Clover, Carol J. and John Lindow, eds. 2005. *Old Norse-Icelandic Literature: A Critical Guide.* Toronto: University of Toronto Press.

de Looze, Laurence, Jón Karl helgason, Russell Poole, and Torfi H. Tulinius, eds. 2015. *Egil, the Viking Poet. New Approaches to Egil's Saga.* Toronto, Buffalo, NY, and London: University of Toronto Press.

Einar Ólafur Sveinsson. 1958. *Dating the Icelandic Sagas: An Essay in Method.* Text Series 3. London: Viking Society for Northern Research.

## Literature    111

Einar Ólafur Sveinsson. 1971 [1943]. *Njáls Saga: A Literary Masterpiece*. Translated by Paul Schach.

Evans, Gareth Lloyd, ed. 2019. *Men and Masculinities in the Sagas of the Icelanders. Oxford English Monographs*. Oxford: Oxford University Press.

Gísli Sigurðsson. 2004. *The Medieval Icelandic Saga and Oral Tradition: A Discourse on Method*. Trans. Nicholas Jones. Cambridge, MA: Harvard University, The Milman Parry Collection of Oral Literature.

Hallberg, Peter. 1962. *The Icelandic Saga*. Trans. with introduction and notes by Paul Schach. Lincoln: University of Nebraska Press.

Haukur Þorgeirsson. 2014. "Snorri Versus the Copyists: An Investigation of a Stylistic Trait in the Manuscript Traditions of *Egils Saga*, *Heimskringla* and the *Prose Edda*". *Saga-Book* XXXVIII: 62–74.

Jóhanna Katrín Friðriksdóttir. 2013. *Women in Old Norse Literature. Bodies, Words, and Power*. New York: Palgrave Macmillan.

Jóhanna Katrín Friðriksdóttir. 2020. 'Manuscripts and Codicology'. In Massimiliano Bampi, Carolyne Larrington, and Sif Rikhardsdottir (eds.): *A Critical Companion to Old Norse Literary Genre*. Cambridge: Cambridge University Press, 89–112.

Jón Jóhannesson. 1974. *A History of the Old Icelandic Commonwealth*. Trans. Haraldur Bessason. Winnipeg: University of Manitoba Press.

Jónas Kristjánsson. 1988. *Eddas and Sagas: Iceland's Medieval Literature*. Trans. Peter Foote. Reykjavík: Hið íslenzka bókmenntafélag.

Lassen, Annette. 2019. "Perseverance and Purity in *Flóamanna Saga*". *Journal of English and Germanic Philology* 118/3: 313–328

Lassen, Annette. 2022. *Odin's Ways: A Guide to the Pagan God in Medieval Literature*. London: Routledge.

Lassen, Annette. 2022. "Kaos og kapital – Et tredje monster i islændingesagaerne?". *Arkiv för nordisk filologi* 137: 1–26.

McTurk, Rory, ed. 2005. *A Companion to Old Norse-Icelandic Literature and Culture*. Oxford: Blackwell Publishing.

Meulengracht Sorensen, Preben. 1983. *The Unmanly Man: Concepts of Sexual Defamation in Early Northern Society*. Trans. Joan Turville-Petre. Odense: Odense University Press.

Miller, William Ian. 1990. *Bloodtaking and Peacemaking. Feud, Law, and Society in Saga Iceland*. Chicago, IL and London: The University of Chicago Press.

Mundal, Else, ed. 2013. *Dating the Sagas*. Copenhagen: Museum Tusculanum Press.

O'Donoghue, Heather. 2021. *Narrative in the Icelandic Family Saga. Meanings of Time in Old Norse Literature*. London, New York, Oxford, New Delhi, and Sydney: Bloomsbury.

O'Donoghue, Heather and Eleanor Parker, eds. 2024. The Cambridge History of Old Norse Icelandic Literature. Cambridge: Cambridge University Press.

Phelpstead, Carl. 2020. *An Introduction to the Sagas of Icelanders*. Gainsville: University Press of Florida.

Poole, Russell, ed. 2001. *Skaldsagas: Text, Vocation and Desire in the Icelandic Sagas of Poets. Reallexikon der germanischen Altertumskunde, Ergänzungsbände*. Berlin and New York: de Gruyter.

Pulsiano, Phillip and Kirsten Wolf, eds. 1993. *Medieval Scandinavia: An Encyclopedia*. New York: Garland.

## 112  *Literature*

Ross, Margaret Clunies 1998. *Prolonged Echoes: Old Norse Myths in Medieval Northern Society. Vol 2: The Reception of Norse Myths in Medieval Iceland.* Odense: Odense University Press.

Ross, Margaret Clunies, ed. 2000. *Old Icelandic Literature and Society.* Cambridge: Cambridge University Press.

Ross, Margaret Clunies. 2010. *The Cambridge Introduction to the Old Norse-Icelandic Saga.* Cambridge: Cambridge University Press.

Sif Rikharðsdóttir. 2017. *Emotion in Old Norse Literature: Translations, Voices, Contexts.* Cambridge: D.S. Brewer.

Sigurður Nordal. 1958 [1940]. *Hrafnkels Saga Freysgoða.* Trans. R. George Thomas. Cardiff: University of Wales.

Sävborg, Daniel. 2012. "The Dating of the Post-Classical Family Saga". *Arkiv för nordisk filologi* 127: 19–57.

Sävborg, Daniel and Karen Bek-Pedersen, eds. 2014. *Folklore in Old Norse – Old Norse in Folkore. Nordistica Tatruensia 20.* Tartu: University of Tartu Press.

Simek, Rudolf and Hermann Pálsson. 1987. *Lexikon der altnordischen Literatur.* Stuttgart: Kröner.

Tucker, John, ed. 1989. *Sagas of the Icelanders: A Book of Essays.* New York: Garland.

Turville-Petre, Gabriel. 1953. *Origins of Icelandic Literature.* Oxford: Clarendon Press.

Vésteinn Ólason. 1998. *Dialogues with the Viking Age: Narration and Representation in the Sagas of the Icelanders.* Trans. Andrew Wawn. Reykjavík: Heimskringla.

# Index

*Alexanders saga* 6
*Arinbjarnarkviða see Arinbjorn's poem*
*Arinbjorn's poem* 43, 76
Ari Þorgilsson, the Learned 1, 5, 21, 26, 49
Árni Magnússon 3, 8–9, 102
*Auðunar þáttr vestfirzka see The Tale of Audun from the West Fjords*

*Bandamanna saga see The Saga of the Confederates*
*Bárðar saga Snæfellsáss see Bard's Saga*
*Bard's Saga (Bárðar saga Snæfellsáss)* 12, 15–16, 18, 32, 46, 74–75
Battle of Clontarf 27, 32, 104
*Beowulf* 86
Bergthorshvol (Bergþórshvoll) 27, 46, 81–82
*Bjarnar saga Hítdælakappa see The Saga of Bjorn, Champion of the Hitardal People*
*Bolla þáttr Bollasonar see Bolli Bollason's tale*
*Bolli Bollason's tale (Bolla þáttr Bollasonar)* 9, 35, 97
*Book of Icelanders (Íslendingabók)* 1, 5, 21, 26–27, 44, 49, 79
*Book of Settlements (Landnámabók)* 1, 12, 18, 20, 23, 26–27, 44, 75–76, 89–91, 94–95, 99, 103
*Book of Settlements (Sturlubók)* 12, 20, 23, 27, 89–90, 95
*Brennu-Njáls saga see Njal's Saga*
Brother Robert (bróðir Róbert) 5

Chrétien de Troyes 5
*Clári saga see The Saga of Klarus*

Denmark 23, 68, 73, 78, 91
*Droplaugarsona saga see The Saga of Droplaug's Sons*

*Edda* (Snorri Sturluson's *Edda*) 1, 11, 20, 27, 72–73, 80–81, 88
*Egil's Saga (Egils saga Skallagrímssonar)* 3, 8–9, 11–12, 14, 31, 36, 40–42, 57, 62–63, 68, 73, 75–76, 97
*Egils saga Skallagrímssonar see Egil's Saga*
Eirik Blood-axe (Eiríkr blóðox), king 31, 41, 75
*Eiríks saga rauða see Eirik the Red's Saga*
*Eirik the Red's Saga* 12, 28–29, 46, 61, 69, 71, 76–77, 92
England 3, 40, 68, 83
*Eyrbyggja saga see The Saga of the People of Eyri*

*Finnboga saga ramma see The Saga of Finnbogi the Mighty*
*Fljótsdæla saga see The Saga of the People of Fljotsdal*
*Flóamanna saga see The Saga of the People of Floi*
Flugumýri 28
*Fóstbræðra saga see The Saga of the Sworn Brothers*
Frey (Freyr), god 38, 80, 89, 100
*Friðþjófs saga frækna see The Saga of Frithiof the Bold*

Geoffrey Chaucer 7
Geoffrey of Monmouth 5, 34
*Gesta Danorum* ("History of the Danes") *see* Saxo Grammaticus

## 114   Index

Giovanni Boccaccio 7, 86
*Gísla saga Súrssonar see Gisli Sursson's Saga*
*Gisli Sursson's Saga (Gísla saga Súrssonar)* 3, 9–10, 14–15, 33, 37–38, 54–56, 59, 77–78, 84–85, 91
*Gold-Thorir's Saga (Gull-Þóris saga)* 12, 15, 54, 78–79
*The Great Saga of Olaf Tryggvason (Óláfs saga Tryggvasonar en mesta)* 75, 93
Greenland 1, 16, 28–29, 45, 54, 57, 68–69, 74, 76–77, 91–93, 95–96, 102
Gregory's *Dialogues* 7
*Grettis saga sterka see The Saga of Grettir the Strong*
*Grænlendinga saga see The Saga of the Greenlanders*
*Gull-Þóris saga see Gold-Thorir's Saga*
*Gunnars saga Keldugnúpsfífls see The Saga of Gunnar, the Fool of Keldugnup*
*Gunnars þáttr Þiðrandabani see The Tale of Gunnar, the Slayer of Thidrandi*
Gunnhild (Gunnhildr), queen 31, 41, 75
*Gunnlaugs saga ormstungu see The Saga of Gunnlaug Serpent-Tongue*
Götaland, Sweden 46, 100

Haakon Haakonson (Hákon Hákonarson), king 5, 24
*Haakon's Saga (Hákonar saga Hákonarsonar)* 24
*Hákonar saga Hákonarsonar see Haakon's Saga*
*Hálfdanar saga Eysteinssonar see Halfdan Eysteinsson's Saga*
*Halfdan Eysteinsson's Saga (Hálfdanar saga Eysteinssonar)* 79
*Hallfreðar saga vandræðaskálds see The Saga of Hallfred the Troublesome Poet*
Harald Fair-hair (Haraldr hárfagri), king 3, 75, 96, 100, 106
Harald Graafeld (Haraldr gráfeldr), king 95
Harald Hardradi (Haraldr harðráði), king 62
*Harðar saga ok Hólmverja see The Saga of Hord and the People of Holm*
*Hávarðar saga Ísfirðings see The Saga of Havard of Isafjord*
*Head Ransom (Hǫfuðlausn)* 9, 41, 43, 75–76

*Heiðarvíga saga see The Saga of the Slayings on the Heath*
*Heimskringla* 7, 11, 20, 34, 73
*Hen-Thorir's Saga (Hænsa-Þóris saga)* 14, 26, 61–62, 79
*Hervarar saga ok Heiðreks see The Saga of Hervor and Heidrek*
*Historia regum Britanniae* ("History of the British Kings") *see* Geoffrey of Monmouth
*History of the Danes see* Saxo Grammaticus
*Hænsa-Þóris saga see Hen-Thorir's Saga*
Hólar 7, 105
*Hrafnkels saga Freysgoða see The Saga of Hrafnkel Frey's Godi*
*Hrólfs saga kraka see The Saga of Hrolf Kraki*
*Hǫfuðlausn see Head Ransom*

Ireland 3, 32, 40, 44, 68, 97, 104
*Íslendingabók see Book of Icelanders*
*Íslendingadrápa* ("Poem about Icelanders") 100
*Íslendinga saga see The Saga of Icelanders*
*Íslendings þáttr sǫgufróða see The Tale of the Story-Wise Icelander*

*Jokul Buason's Tale (Jǫkuls þáttr Búasonar)* 87, 96
Jón Ǫgmundarson, bishop 7
Jón Ólafsson from Grunnavík 3, 9, 102
*Jóns saga helga see The Saga of St. Jón of Hólar*

*Killer-Glum's saga (Víga-Glúms saga)* 9, 14, 79–80, 98
*Kjalnesinga saga see The Saga of the People of Kjalarnes*
Klœngr Þorsteinsson, bishop 7
*Kormak's saga (Kormáks saga)* 9, 12, 40, 54, 58, 68, 80–81
*Kristni þáttr see The Tale about Christianity*
*Kristni saga see The Saga of the Conversion*
*Króka-Refs saga see The Saga of Ref the Sly*

*Landnámabók see Book of Settlements*
L'Anse aux Meadows 29, 76, 92

*Index* 115

*Lausavísur* 9, 41, 76
*Laxdœla saga see The Saga of the People of Laxardal*
*Ljósvetninga saga see The Saga of the People of Ljosavatn*
*Lokasenna see Loki's Quarrel*
*Loki's Quarrel (Lokasenna)* 82,
*Loss of Sons (Sonatorrek)* 9, 40, 42–43, 75–76

Magnus Lawmender (Magnús lagabœtir), king 23–24
*Magnus Lawmender's Saga (Magnúss saga lagabœtis)* 23

*Njal's Saga (Brennu-Njáls saga)* 3–4, 6–9, 14–15, 27–29, 32–33, 35–39, 44, 46–47, 50–53, 55, 57, 67, 81–82, 95–97, 103, 105
Norway 3, 31, 44, 46, 47, 53, 60–62, 68, 71, 74–75, 77–80, 83–89, 91–93, 95–96, 99–104, 106

Oddr Snorrason, monk 5–7, 16, 34
Odin (Óðinn), god 16, 42–43, 46, 74, 90
*Ófeigs þáttr see The Tale of Ofeig*
Olaf Haraldsson the Saint (Óláfr Haraldsson inn helgi), king 31, 35, 74, 83, 86, 102–103
*Óláfsmáldagi* ("Olaf's inventory") 10
*Óláfs saga helga see The Saga of Saint Olaf*
*Óláfs saga Tryggvasonar see The Saga of Olaf Tryggvason*
*Óláfs saga Tryggvasonar en mesta see The Great Saga of Olaf Tryggvason*
Olaf Tryggvason (Óláfr Tryggvason), king 43, 46–48, 72–73, 76, 88, 93
*Olkofri's Saga (Ǫlkofra saga)* 9, 13, 82
Orkney Islands 3, 41, 44, 104
*Orms þáttr Stórólfssonar see Orm Storolfsson's Tale*
*Orm Storolfsson's Tale (Orms þáttr Stórólfssonar)* 72
Ovid: *Ars amatoria (Art of love)* 7

*Ragnars saga loðbrókar see The Saga of Ragnar Lothbrok*
*Reykdœla saga ok Víga-Skútu see The Saga of the People of Reykjadal and of Killer-Skuta*

*The Saga of Bjorn, Champion of the Hitardal People (Bjarnar saga Hítdœlakappa)* 9, 12, 31, 40, 58, 63–64, 83, 87, 103
*The Saga of Droplaug's Sons (Droplaugarsona saga)* 9, 12, 19, 33, 83–84, 94–95, 100
*The Saga of Finnbogi the Mighty (Finnboga saga ramma)* 9, 15, 31, 35, 71, 85, 100
*The Saga of Frithiof the Bold (Friðþjófs saga frœkna)* 80, 106
*The Saga of Grettir the Strong (Grettis saga sterka)* 7, 12, 15, 20, 32, 36, 38, 69–71, 73, 85–86
*The Saga of Gunnlaug Serpent-Tongue (Gunnlaugs saga ormstungu)* 14, 20–21, 40–41, 58, 83, 87–88, 104
*The Saga of Hallfred the Troublesome Poet (Hallfreðar saga vandrœðaskálds)* 9, 12, 40, 43, 58, 68–69, 88, 95
*The Saga of Havard of Isafjord (Hávarðar saga Ísfirðings)* 12, 15, 62, 89, 91
*The Saga of Hervor and Heidrek (Hervarar saga ok Heiðreks)* 103
*The Saga of Hrafnkel Frey's Godi (Hrafnkels saga Freysgoða)* 3, 6, 14–15, 17–18, 38, 57, 89–90, 94–95
*The Saga of Hrolf Kraki (Hrólfs saga kraka)* 103
*The Saga of Hord and the People of Holm (Harðar saga ok Hólmverja)* 12, 15–16, 32, 46, 90
*The Saga of Icelanders, by Sturla Þórðarson (Íslendinga saga)* 10, 28
*The Saga of Klarus (Clári saga)* 22
*The Saga of Olaf Tryggvason (Óláfs saga Tryggvasonar)* 6–7, 34, 48, 75, 93
*The Saga of Ragnar Lothbrok, (Ragnars saga loðbrókar)* 103
*The Saga of Ref the Sly (Króka-Refs saga)* 15–16, 91
*The Saga of Saint Olaf (Óláfs saga helga)* 14, 83
*The Saga of St. Jón of Hólar (Jóns saga helga)* 7
*The Saga of the Confederates (Bandamanna saga)* 9, 12, 14, 50, 82, 91–92
*The Saga of the Conversion (Kristni saga)* 27

## 116   Index

*The Saga of the Greenlanders*
  (*Grœnlendinga saga*) 13, 28–29,
  76–77, 92–93
*The Saga of Gunnar, the Fool*
  *of Keldugnup* (*Gunnars saga*
  *Keldugnúpsfifls*) 15–16, 86–87
*The Saga of the People of Eyri* (*Eyrbyggja*
  *saga*) 3, 8–9, 11, 14, 20, 32, 37, 45,
  67–68, 83, 93–94, 101
*The Saga of the People of Fljotsdal*
  (*Fljótsdœla saga*) 9, 15, 25, 44, 84–85,
  90, 94–95
*The Saga of the People of Floi*
  (*Flóamanna saga*) 15–16, 32, 45,
  57–58, 71, 95–96
*The Saga of the People of Kjalarnes*
  (*Kjalnesinga saga*) 15, 44, 74, 87,
  91, 96
*The Saga of the People of Laxardal*
  (*Laxdœla saga*) 3–5, 8, 9, 11, 14,
  32–33, 35–37, 44–45, 49–53, 58, 62,
  66, 68, 71, 76, 83, 85, 87, 93–97, 101,
  103–104
*The Saga of the People of Ljosavatn*
  (*Ljósvetninga saga*) 13, 67, 97–98, 105
*The Saga of the People of Reykjadal and*
  *of Killer-Skuta* (*Reykdœla saga ok*
  *Víga-Skútu*) 13, 21, 58, 80, 98
*The Saga of the People of Svarfadardal*
  (*Svarfdœla saga*) 12, 15, 17, 21–22,
  32, 98, 105
*The Saga of the People of Vatnsdal*
  (*Vatnsdœla saga*) 3, 14, 32, 44, 54, 85,
  99–100
*The Saga of the People of Vopnafjord*
  (*Vápnfirðinga saga*) 4, 13, 35, 44, 50,
  85, 100–101, 104
*The Saga of the Slayings on the Heath*
  (*Heiðarvíga saga*) 6, 8, 11–12, 54, 68,
  94, 101–102
*The Saga of the Sturlungs* (*Sturlunga*
  *saga*) 23
*The Saga of the Sworn Brothers*
  (*Fóstbrœðra saga*) 9, 12–13, 24–25,
  30–31, 33–36, 40, 53–54, 68–69,
  102–103
*The Saga of Thord Menace* (*Þórðar saga*
  *hreðu*) 15, 91, 103
*The Saga of Thorstein the White*
  (*Þorsteins saga hvíta*) 14, 83, 87, 95,
  100, 104

Saxo Grammaticus 5, 16, 23, 33
Skálholt 7
Snorri Sturluson 1, 11, 20, 24, 27, 34,
  72–73, 75, 80–81, 88
*Sonatorrek see Loss of Sons*
*Sǫrla þáttr see The Tale of Sorli*
*Spesar þáttr see The Tale about Spes*
Sturla Þórðarson 10–12, 23–25, 27,
  89–90, 95
*Sturlu þáttr see The Tale of Sturla*
*Sturlunga saga see The Saga of the*
  *Sturlungs*
*Svarfdœla saga see The Saga of the*
  *People of Svarfadardal*
Sweden 3, 8–9, 41, 46, 88, 90, 102

*The Tale about Christianity* (*Kristni þáttr*)
  46, 82
*The Tale about Spes* (*Spesar þáttr*) 86
*The Tale of Audun from the West Fjords*
  ·(*Auðunar þáttr vestfirzka*) 62, 68, 91
*The Tale of Gunnar, the Slayer*
  *of Thidrandi* (*Gunnars þáttr*
  *Þiðrandabani*) 94–95
*The Tale of Ofeig* (*Ófeigs þáttr*) 98
*The Tale of Ogmund Bash* (*Ǫgmundar*
  *þáttr dytts ok Gunnars helmings*) 61
*The Tale of Sorli* (*Sǫrla þáttr*) 98
*The Tale of Sturla* (*Sturlu þáttr*) 23
*The Tale of the Story-Wise Icelander*
  (*Íslendings þáttr sǫgufróða*) 25
*The Tale of Thorvald the Far-Travelled*
  (*Þorvalds þáttr víðfǫrla*) 48, 100
*The Tale of Vodu-Brand* (*Vǫðu-Brands*
  *þáttr*) 98
Thor (*Þórr*), god 16, 45, 54, 77, 93, 95
Thorlak (*Þórlákr helgi Þórhallson*), saint
  45, 95, 101
*Thorstein Sidu-Hallsson's Saga* (*Þorsteins*
  *saga Síðu-Hallssonar*)
*Tristram* 5

*Vápnfirðinga saga see The Saga of the*
  *People of Vopnafjord*
*Vatnsdœla saga see The Saga of the*
  *People of Vatnsdal*
*Viga-Glúms saga see Killer-Glum's saga*
Vinland (*Vínland*) 1, 29, 46, 68, 76–77,
  92–93
*Vǫðu-Brands þáttr see The Tale of*
  *Vodu-Brand*

*Index*  117

Þingeyrar 5
*Þórðar saga hreðu see The Saga of Thord
Menace*
*Þorsteins saga hvíta see The Saga of
Thorstein the White*
*Þorsteins saga Síðu-Hallssonar see
Thorstein Sidu-Hallsson's Saga*

*Þorvalds þáttr viðforla see The Tale of
Thorvald the Far-Travelled*

*Ǫgmundar þáttr dytts ok Gunnars
helmings see The Tale of Ogmund
Bash*
*Ǫlkofra saga see Olkofri's Saga*

# Index of Manuscripts

**Copenhagen**
*The Arnamagnæan Collection,*
*Department of Nordic and*
*Linguistic Studies, University of*
*Copenhagen*
AM 226 fol. (ca. 1350-1360) 6
AM 309 4to (1498) 94
AM 453 4to (seventeenth century) 75
AM 468 4to (ca. 1300-1325)
Reykjabók 6, 8, 81–82
AM 544 4to (ca. 1300) (Hauksbók)
13, 76–77, 103
Hauksbók *see* AM 544 4to
Reykjabók *see* AM 468 4to

**Reykjavík**
*The Árni Magnússon Institute for*
*Icelandic Studies, University of*
*Iceland*
AM 132 fol. (ca. 1330-1370)
(Möðruvallabók) 8–9, 35, 75, 80–
82, 84–85, 88, 92, 95, 97, 103
AM 133 fol. (ca. 1350)
(Kálfalækjarbók) 47, 82
AM 142 fol. (1690-1697) 105
AM 156 fol. (ca. 1650) 87, 104
AM 158 fol. (ca. 1630-1675) 75
AM 160 fol. (seventeenth century) 89
AM 161 fol. (seventeenth century)
99, 106
AM 162 A Φ fol. (ca. 1250) 76
AM 162 C fol. (ca. 1420-1450) 85,
101
AM 162 C 1 fol. (ca. 1420-1450) 98
AM 162 E fol. (ca. 1300) 94
AM 162 F fol. (ca. 1350-1400) 83

AM 162 G fol. (ca. 1400-1500) 79
AM 162 I fol. (ca. 1500) 90
AM 164 h fol. (seventeenth century)
96
Flateyjarbók see GKS 1005 fol.
GKS 1005 fol. (ca. 1387–1395)
(Flateyjarbók) 16, 30–31, 33–36,
88, 93, 103
Kálfalækjarbók *see* AM 133 fol.
Möðruvallabók *see* AM 132 fol.
AM 443 4to (seventeenth century) 87
AM 445 b 4to (ca. 1390-1425
(Pseudo-Vatnshyrna) 94–95, 100
AM 445 c I 4to (ca. 1390-1425)
(Pseudo-Vatnshyrna) 10, 78, 80
AM 445 c II 4to (ca. 1450) 99
AM 448 4to (ca. 1700) 94
AM 450 b 4to (1730) 102
AM 453 4to (seventeenth century) 75
AM 471 4to (ca. 1450-1500) 91, 96
AM 486 4to (seventeenth
century) 75
AM 496 4to (ca. 1640) 87, 104, 106
AM 504 4to (seventeenth century) 96
AM 510 4to (ca. 1550) 85, 106
AM 516 4to (seventeenth century) 96
AM 517 4to (ca. 1700) 96
AM 551 a 4to (ca. 1500) 106
AM 551 c 4to (ca. 1630-1640) 95
AM 551 d β 4to (ca. 1400-1450) 103
AM 554 i 4to (seventeenth century)
87
AM 556 a 4to (ca. 1475-1500) 78,
86, 90
AM 557 4to (ca. 1420-1450)
(Skálholtsbók) 88

## 120   Index of Manuscripts

AM 560 c 4to (1700-1725) 96
AM 561 4to (ca. 1400) 79, 98
AM 564 a 4to (ca. 1390-1425)
  (Pseudo-Vatnshyrna) 75, 80, 90, 103
GKS 2845 4to (ca. 1450) 92
GKS 2870 4to (ca. 1300)
  (Gráskinna) 82
Gráskinna *see* GKS 2870 4to
Skálholtsbók *see* AM 557 4to

*National and University Library of*
*Iceland*

JS 435 4to (1687-1877?) 105
Lbs frg 1 (1300-1350) 102

**Stockholm**
*Royal library*
  Holm perg 18 4to (ca. 1300-1350)
  88, 102

**Wolfenbüttel**
*Herzog August Bibliothek*
  WolfAug 9 10 4to (ca. 1330-1370)
  94

Printed in the United States
by Baker & Taylor Publisher Services